ON THE SLOW TRAIN AGAIN

Michael Williams writes widely on railways for many publications, including the *Daily Mail*, *Independent*, *Independent on Sunday*, *New Statesman*, *Oldie* and the railway specialist press. He is a veteran Fleet Street journalist, having held many senior positions, including Deputy Editor of the *Independent on Sunday*, Executive Editor of the *Independent* and Head of News at the *Sunday Times*. He is currently Senior Lecturer in the School of Journalism, Media and Communication at the University of Central Lancashire. He commutes regularly by train on the 440-mile return journey between his home in London's Camden Town and his office at Preston in Lancashire.

Also by Michael Williams

On the Slow Train

ON THE SLOW TRAIN AGAIN

Michael Williams

arrow books

Published by Arrow 2012

10 9 8 7 6 5 4 3 2 1

Copyright © Michael Williams 2011, 2012

First published in Great Britain in 2011 by Preface Publishing

20 Vauxhall Bridge Road
London, SW1V 2SA

An imprint of The Random House Group Limited

www.randomhouse.co.uk

Addresses for companies within The Random House Group Limited
can be found at www.randomhouse.co.uk

The Random House Group Limited Reg. No. 954009

A CIP catalogue record for this book is available from the British Library

ISBN 978 0 09955 285 7

The Random House Group Limited supports The Forest Stewardship Council (FSC®), the
leading international forest certification organisation. Our books carrying the FSC label are
printed on FSC® certified paper. FSC is the only forest certification scheme endorsed by
the leading environmental organisations, including Greenpeace. Our paper procurement
policy can be found at www.randomhouse.co.uk/environment

Typeset in Perpetua by Palimpsest Book Production Limited,
Falkirk, Stirlingshire
Printed and bound by CPI Group (UK) Ltd, Croydon, CR0 4YY

CONTENTS

An English idyll: Nothing better symbolises the golden age of
the railway than a stopping train in the countryside on an early
summer's day. Here GWR 0-4-2T No. 1472 leaves St Mary's
Crossing Halt in Gloucestershire's Golden Valley on 25 May 1963,
the year Beeching swung his axe.

ON THE SLOW TRAIN AGAIN

There are few love affairs more passionate than that of the British with their railways. We invented the passenger train, and pride in the great heroes of the railway era – the Stephensons, Trevithick, Brunel – runs through our national DNA. No wonder we were all so traumatised nearly fifty years ago, when a plump balding physicist with an authoritarian moustache and an obsession with the bottom line took an axe to a third of Britain's rail network. Dr Richard Beeching had been recruited from the chemicals industry to produce his infamous 1963 report, *The Reshaping of British Railways*, and his proposals were draconian. Most stopping trains would be discontinued. Some 2,350 stations would be shut, along with 5,000 miles of track. No area would be spared. Almost all of Devon, Lincolnshire, Cumbria, Wales and the Highlands of Scotland would be robbed entirely of their passenger train services.

The arguments about Beeching still rage on half a century later. Did he deploy his brilliant scientific background to drag an inefficient nationalised industry out of the steam age and into the modern era? Or was he, as the *Daily Mail* writer Quentin Letts recently claimed, a 'foolish slasher-and-burner', who dumped our railway heritage into the bin like cold leftovers? As it turned out, the plans of the 'evil doctor' were widely implemented – the closure notices went up and a mood of sadness descended across the land. There was no more eloquent expression of the sense of national hurt than Michael Flanders and Donald Swann's famous song, 'Slow Train', from which this book derives its title. Their litany of quaint-sounding stations facing closure was a requiem for the passing of an era: 'No one departs and no one arrives / From Selby to Goole, from St Erth to St Ives. / They've all passed out of our lives . . .'

This volume of journeys is a celebration of the slow trains of Britain that lived on against the odds – and continue to thrive in the twenty-first century. Fortunately, Beeching's cold accountant's logic did not always prevail, and like the villagers of Titfield in the famous Ealing comedy *The Titfield Thunderbolt*, communities across the land fought back and frequently won. Many of the loveliest railway journeys across the most scenic and historic landscapes of Britain are still with us, to be enjoyed for the price of an often inexpensive National Rail ticket. In my recent book *On the Slow Train* I invited readers to join me in travelling on twelve of the best of them. But there are many other riches to be shared, and I am delighted to offer a further selection of Britain's best train journeys in this new volume.

Here is the 'train to the end of the world', running for more than four splendid hours through lake, loch and moorland from Inverness to Wick, the most northerly town in Britain. I take the single-carriage train along a perfect country branch line in London's commuterland and join one of the slowest services in the land along the shores of the lovely Dovey estuary to the far west of Wales. I buy a ticket on the stopping train across the Pennines on a line with so few services that its glorious scenery is a secret known only to the regulars. Here too is the Bittern Line in Norfolk and the Tarka Line in north Devon as well as the little branch line to the fishing port of Looe in Cornwall, rescued from closure in the 1960s and now celebrating its 150th anniversary taking families on holiday to the seaside. The journeys range from the most luxurious and historic – aboard the Orient Express – to the most futuristic – on the driverless trains of London's Docklands Light Railway.

There have been many books published about the railways with words in their titles such as 'Glory Days' or 'As It Was' which have a sepia-tinted take on reality: this is not one of them. Rather, these chapters aim to capture the essence of our railway byways in the present-day landscape, especially through the words of the people I encounter on the journey. This is not, however, to overlook the glorious railway heritage that is still here to be enjoyed. Above all, I hope the book conveys the infinite delight of slow travel in a hurried and fretful era. 'There was always more in the world than men could see, walked they ever so slowly; they will see it no better for going fast,' wrote the great Victorian social thinker John Ruskin. 'The really precious things are thought and sight, not pace. It does . . . a man . . . no harm to go slow; for his glory is not at all in going, but in being.' Those modern slow train travellers, Paul Theroux and Michael Palin, put it more pithily. 'Looking out of a train window,' wrote Theroux '. . . is like watching an unedited travelogue, without the obnoxious soundtrack.' For Palin, the mantra is even simpler: 'If travelling's worth doing, it's worth doing in a leisurely manner.'

Home is a good starting point for any exploration, Palin argues. There's no need to travel thousands of miles to exotic places when you have so much on your doorstep. And many of us are increasingly thinking the same way. New figures show that passenger numbers have recently soared on branch lines and small rural railways such as the ones described in this book, with increases of up to ninety per cent. This may reflect the trend towards 'staycations' – staying at home in Britain for our holidays.

All this makes it less likely that, in our environmentally and socially conscious age, there will ever be another Beeching. But who knows? One thing is certain: the communities of Britain will remain on their guard. Like the best love affairs, Britain's attachment to her railways defies explanation and the authorities tinker with it at their peril. 'The curious but intense pleasure that is given to many by railway trains is both an art and a mystery,' wrote the essayist and historian Roger Lloyd. 'It is an art because the pleasure to be had is exactly proportionate to the enthusiasm one puts into it. It is a mystery because it is impossible to explain to others.'

Climb aboard with me and experience the joy of the slow train for yourself.

Sun sets on a railway empire: The year is 1959, when the axe fell on most of the sprawling network of the old Midland and Great Northern Joint Railway, nicknamed the 'Muddle and Get Nowhere'. Fortunately Sheringham station lives on, and can still be reached on a slow train from Norwich.

CHAPTER ONE

THE 14.36 FROM NORWICH – ON THE CRAB AND LOBSTER LINE TO POPPYLAND-BY-THE-SEA

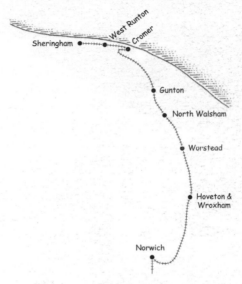

Norwich to Sheringham, via Wroxham, Worstead, Cromer and West Runton

Once upon a time, the departure board at King's Cross station, embarkation point for some of the grandest train journeys in the land, would resonate with the important-sounding names of famous expresses – the Coronation, the Elizabethan, the Talisman, the Fair Maid, the West Riding Limited, the Tyne-Tees Pullman – and, most famous of all, the Flying Scotsman. The least of these – a mouse among the big beasts of the main line – was the Cambridge Buffet Express, introduced in 1932 and soon given the unromantic nickname the Beer Train by thirsty Cambridge undergraduates, who thronged the buffet car to quaff Watney's Pale or Mann's Brown Ale well before the pubs opened at lunchtime.

Most of these celebrated services have passed into history (although the Flying Scotsman name lives on still with the 10 a.m. departure to Edinburgh), and the expresses on the electronic departure board in the concourse this lunchtime are listed unceremoniously by just the names of the cities they serve – Glasgow, Inverness, Newcastle, York, Leeds. But wait. Popping up in bright orange LEDs (the familiar whispering clatter of the mechanical destination board now a thing of past) is the announcement of my own train – the 12.15 to Cambridge and King's Lynn. Not just a train, you understand. THE CAMBRIDGE EXPRESS, the indicator declares importantly, 12.15. PLATFORM 1. As it happens, the Cambridge Express is a rather unassuming train, even by the modest standards of its own heritage, consisting of a suburban electric Networker unit usually employed in shuttling commuters to and from the north London suburbs. There is no buffet, no trolley, and any undergraduate on board panting for a snifter would need to have stocked up in advance at the station Threshers. But let's celebrate that a sentimental heart still beats somewhere in the corporate headquarters of First Capital Connect, the train's operator, and that we are able to take an 'express' at all, since my destination is Norwich, and the trains on the direct line from Liverpool Street are disrupted by engineering work.

The train fairly rattles (in both senses of the word) along the line on its non-stop journey to Cambridge, and it is possible still to derive a little glamour by association, since this is the train the Queen sometimes takes when she travels to Sandringham. In these thrifty days it is good PR for Her Majesty to be seen to travel on a normal service, rather than wheeling out the full pomp of the Royal Train, though her retinue customarily book out an entire first-class section, which is then locked to avoid her encountering gawping commuters –

and one imagines that a Fortnum's hamper is adequate compensation for the lack of a buffet car. For me, there's a swift change of trains at Ely, one of the nicest stations on the network, with the great square tower of the Norman cathedral looming over a green landscape rendered even more charming on this late spring afternoon by an archery competition taking place in the field alongside the tracks. The main line across the Fens to Norwich is one of the most delightful in Britain, still staffed by signallers pulling primitive wires to operate traditional semaphore signals in Victorian wooden signal boxes at places called Shippea Hill, Lakenheath, Thetford, Harling Road, Eccles Road, Attleborough, Spooner Row and Wymondham. Enjoy the atmosphere while you can, since the signals are due to be dismantled and replaced with an electronic system by 2013. Soon I am at Norwich, with a minute to spare for my branch line train north to the coast along the Bittern Line to Sheringham.

There's an irony here since the Bittern Line, running for thirty and a half miles through the Broads to the north Norfolk seaside, offers many things – ancient landscapes, historic houses and churches, ravishing vistas across unspoilt wetlands and pretty Victorian seaside resorts – but you will be lucky to see the bird that gives the line its name. This small heron-like creature is one of Britain's rarest breeding birds – on an average winter fewer than a hundred specimens are recorded throughout the country. Twitchers (bird watchers, who must not be confused with gricers, who are trainspotters) stalk the Norfolk reed beds in the hope of catching the sound of the bittern's famous *boom*. The bird's cry is the lowest-pitched and furthest-carrying song of any European bird, audible more than three miles away. But we are unlikely to hear the sound today, even if a flock of bitterns were perched on a platform fence, since, in common with many British branch line trains, our 1980s Class 156 two-carriage diesel train has noisy underfloor engines and screeching wheels.

But who cares? The compensations are abundant as we pull out over the points from Norwich Thorpe. How many other railways in Europe link a historic medieval city, a national park and an area of outstanding natural beauty, along with some of the nation's most unspoilt seaside resorts, over such a brief distance? And how many departures from city stations have been celebrated in classics of children's literature? A journey beginning at Norwich Thorpe station was the introduction to Dick and Dorothea Callum's Broadland holiday adventure in Arthur Ransome's 1934 novel *Coot Club*. It might have been a proud LNER Sandringham Class steam engine on the front in those days, but the scene is the same today. 'They crossed a bridge,' wrote Ransome, 'and there was the river on both sides of the line, the old river on the left curving round by the village of Thorpe with crowds of yachts and cabin cruisers tied up under the gardens.'

There's a carnival atmosphere on the train this afternoon, as we rattle north over the points at Whitlingham Junction. (Whitlingham willows are renowned for putting the spring into many a Test match cricket bat.) Arthur, the conductor, explains that there's a specially cheery crowd aboard this afternoon because Norwich folk are travelling down to Cromer for the annual Crab and Lobster Festival on the coast. Lucky old Cromer, since the weather for a Whitsun weekend is uncharacteristically hot. It is exactly fifty-two years ago to the day that Philip Larkin wrote 'Whitsun Weddings', one of the most famous railway poems of all, as he took a journey on a similarly warm afternoon out of Hull, where he was the university's librarian. 'All windows down, all cushions hot,' he wrote as his train pulled slowly through the eastern counties on its journey to London.

Today the seats are hot all right, but our train has neither air conditioning, nor, as in Larkin's day, those old-fashioned windows with leather straps that would drop down to let in a waft of spring air. But the views are magnificent as we climb past the Norwich fringes and into open countryside, with the froth of may and cherry blossom everywhere, exuberant after one of the harshest winters for more than half a century. Overgrown line-side vegetation whips against the side of the train, and it is easy to forget that until Beeching had his way the Bittern Line was an important main line from London, with named expresses such as the Broadsman, the East Anglian and the Norfolkman, speeding eager families to the resorts and holiday camps of the Norfolk coast in the days when Torremolinos and Benidorm were just exotic names in a school atlas.

The railways of East Anglia were especially badly savaged by the cuts of the 1950s and 1960s, and the Bittern Line is the last surviving branch line on the national network north from Norwich. No longer do slow trains clatter into the platform at Snettisham, Fakenham and Potter Heigham. The days when it was possible to buy a day return from Whitwell & Reepham to Hindolveston or Melton Constable, or an arthritic porter incanted the names of little stations from Martham (for Rollesby) to Paston & Knapton, are fast fading from memory.

Such was the speed of the railway mania of the nineteenth century (and the social change that was swept along with it) that within fifty years of the opening of the Stockton and Darlington Railway in the heart of the industrial north, almost nobody even in rural East Anglia was more than five miles from a railway station. The problem was that there was no central strategy and no planning. Minor railways were built, not because there was anyone in particular to use them, but as a way of stopping rivals encroaching on your turf. For the best part of eighty years this did not matter. As John Brodribb, historian of the east of England's railways, comments in his book *Branches and Byways – East Anglia,* 'the railways became an unchanging fixed part of the fabric of rural life: people set their clocks by them, went to school, went to war, went to get married on them. If only . . .'

If only. Until the hatchet men and bean counters came along in the 1960s, nobody seemed to have noticed that Norfolk's branch lines were being used by very few people. The truth was – and utter it quietly – few local lines had ever, in their history, been used much at all. The axe fell swiftly on most, and the main line to Cromer, along which our train is sashaying this afternoon, was downgraded to a branch. But at least it survived.

Salhouse, the first stop out of Norwich, is just the sort of quiet village that would have lost its services had it not been on the route of the old main line. As it is, there is not much here except memories. Although one of the brick station buildings from the original East Norfolk Railway survives, with cheery Victorian cast iron spandrels supporting the canopy, the waiting room and the cubbyhole where porters supped their tea between trains is now boarded up, although someone has taken the trouble to fill the platform tubs with violas and there is lilac tumbling over the platform fence. There are other ghosts too. When the journalist Alexander Frater came this way in the 1980s for his book *Stopping Train Britain* he observed that during World War II there had been more than eighty airfields in East Anglia, and Salhouse was one of them. In Frater's time many railway staff still had memories of the war, and his train driver, Reg Reynolds, told him, 'Just over there, beyond the fence, was where they parked *F for Freddie*. The crew always waved when we steamed past. I remember those young chaps in their sheepskin jackets smiling and waving. After each mission they painted a white bomb on the nose of the plane, and we used to count those bombs and wonder how long their luck would last. Well, it lasted up to the seventeenth white bomb and we never saw them again.'

This is gentle country. As we head down the gradient to the next stop at Hoveton & Wroxham – 'the gateway to the Broads' – a pair of red admiral butterflies bump against the window and a hare kicks its heels away from the train. This is the classic East Anglian landscape celebrated by Adrian Bell, who wrote his 'Countryman's Notebook' column in the local *East Anglian Daily Times* for thirty years as well as twenty books about the countryside hereabouts. Never heard of Adrian Bell? His son Martin Bell, the BBC war reporter, still flies the family standard for journalism. Back in 1934 Arthur Ransome wrote of Dick and Dorothea Callum's approach to Wroxham in *Coot Club*, 'The train was slowing up. It crossed another river and for a moment they caught a glimpse of moored houseboats with smoke from their chimneys where people were cooking midday meals, an old mill and a bridge with lots of masts behind it. And then the train came to a stop . . .' There's still an old wooden signal box here that Dick and Dorothea might recognise – the last one remaining on the line – being restored with money from the Railway Heritage Trust. It looks odd, being painted in what appear to be the chocolate and cream colours of the Great Western Railway. But one of the workmen taking a rest on the platform tells me these were also the colours used on the line in the Great Eastern Railway days of yore.

Today the train fills up with teenagers from a less innocent age, swigging Slush Puppies and chattering over the sound of iPods firmly clamped to ears. There's some tut-tutting from some of the oldies in the Cromer festival crowd, but young passengers are the lifeblood of lines such as this, in country areas where local buses are few and the wait for a driving licence at seventeen seems interminable. Hoveton and Wroxham are two villages on either side of the River Bure, which used to be navigable as far as the neighbouring town of Aylsham, but these days it is better to change onto the little narrow-gauge steam train that chugs along the trackbed of the closed branch line that ran between Wroxham and County School on the Wymondham to Wells-next-the-Sea railway — another Beeching victim. One of the little 15-inch gauge engines, polished and burnished like a blackberry, is simmering alluringly on the turntable, ready to take its next train back to Aylsham, traversing Norfolk's only railway tunnel on the way. But I must get on, because the lobsters and crabs of Cromer cannot wait.

As we head north from Hoveton & Wroxham, sheep form little white dots across the landscape as far as the eye can see, a sight that has greeted travellers over millennia, since we are approaching Worstead, where the famous worsted cloth was first spun in the twelfth century by weavers from Flanders. (Not a spellcheck error. Both versions are correct, deriving from the Anglo-Saxon name Wrdesteda, as it appears in the Domesday Book.) Here, visible along the line, crowning the flat landscape, is a series of fine churches created by the prosperity of the wool trade. First, St Swithin's, Ashman-haugh, whose round tower is the narrowest in England. Then there is St Mary's, Tunstead, with its magnificent medieval rood screen, and St Bartholomew's, Sloley, so close to the track that you could almost reach out and touch the mossy headstones in the graveyard. Grandest of all is St Mary's, Worstead, a mile from the station, whose tower dominates the landscape with greater presence than many an English cathedral.

Don't alight at Worstead hoping to take some of its famous cloth home with you: it hasn't been made here for more than a century. The last weaver John Cubitt died in 1882 aged ninety-one. But the village itself is as nice as you will find anywhere in rural England, and worsted is still produced in the UK, especially in mills around Huddersfield, and remains one of the most desirable fabrics in the world. Why is it so special? Ask the Prince of Wales, David Beckham, and the royalty of the Premier League who buy their bespoke worsted suits in Savile Row, where prices are £4,000 upwards. The secret, apparently, lies in the long fibres woven into parallel lines, giving the cloth an ability to 'bounce back' – certainly better than the England football team's performance over recent years.

The next station, North Walsham, still has long platforms dating from the days when the Norfolk Coast Express and the Broadsman, complete with restaurant car, drew up importantly here on their way from Liverpool Street. But no original buildings remain, just some scantily constructed bus shelters – the signature of post-Beeching stations across the land. Arthur hops onto the platform for a natter with the driver, in time-honoured branch line idiom, as we wait for a southbound train to trundle off the single-track section ahead. In a siding a maroon and gold Class 66 freight diesel thrums gently in the hot afternoon at the head of a train of tanker wagons. The railwaymen explain that this is the last daily freight train left in rural Norfolk, where hundreds of sugar beet trains once ran, and contains condensate – a by-product of the North Sea gas industry, which is taken by train from here to Harwich for processing. 'They'll never close this bit. It's strat-eee-gic, see,' Arthur tells me in his slow Norfolk accent, explaining that liquid gas is piped from the North Sea to the North Walsham rail terminal. 'Essential for the security of our fuel supplies,' the other man tells me conspiratorially, with an age-old gesture to the side of his nose.

But suddenly it's getting busy as a third train arrives, bound for Norwich, bearing a jumble of liveries – one coach in the grey and white colours of National Express, the operator of the line, and another bearing the lime-green insignia of Central Trains, a franchise that no longer exists. All very jolly, and a reminder, in the modern era of corporate identity and focus groups, of the pre-grouping era before 1923, when many branch lines were operated by a ragbag of colourful coaches pensioned off from the main lines to see out their dotage in forgotten parts of the countryside. North Walsham was once famous for another collection of old carriages – the camping coaches popular in the 1930s and in 1950s austerity Britain, which offered cheap holidays and a touch of adventure for small children whose families could not run to a seaside hotel, as well as providing a useful after-life for rolling stock too decrepit for its wheels to turn any longer. The station sidings here were once in the record books as the location of the biggest collection of camping coaches in the country. However, camping coach holidays were not all romance – as I discovered as a boy during a family holiday at the end of a siding at Felixstowe, not far from here. The carriage may have once passed its days glamorously as part of crack expresses from King's Cross, but the most enduring memory for me was the ripe odour of the chemical toilet, which had to be emptied in the station gents every day. North Walsham has another more conventional claim to fame – as the place where Lord Nelson went to school between 1768 and 1771. Paston Grammar School is still open for business, and its playing fields are just across the road from the station.

No such privations at the next stop, Gunton, where the buildings on the northbound platform have been splendidly restored, and are in use as a private house. With original cast iron signs marked PORTER and STATION MASTER, red fire buckets and enamel advertisements for Colman's Starch and 'Corona Sparkling Drinks and Squashes – Drink all the Year Round', it is straight out of the *Antiques Roadshow* and won a National Railway Heritage Award in 2009 – although this may not be much consolation to passengers, who must huddle in a single bus shelter on the bare platform opposite as they observe enviously the elegant interior decorations through the windows. The building was originally the best appointed of all the stations on the line, since it was

equipped to cater for royal visitors dropping in to see Lord
Suffield, one of the biggest investors in the building of the
line, at his lovely home at Gunton Hall nearby. Indeed Stanley
Hurn, the present owner and the man who restored the
station, is himself a potentate of the modern age as a distinguished international banker and freeman of the City of
London.

Soon we pass a weed-covered embankment curving away to
the left, where the expresses once headed direct to Sheringham,
but so many tracks have been lifted in these parts that our
train will have to undertake a complicated reversal to get there.
There is no mistaking the approach to Cromer. The tower of
the church of St Peter and St Paul soars over the town, and
at 160 feet is the tallest in Norfolk. In the minds of railway
enthusiasts, Cromer station has a similarly exalted status as
one of only three surviving on the national network from the
days of the fabled Midland and Great Northern Joint Railway.
Like that other legendary joint line, the Somerset and Dorset,
the 'Muddle and Get Nowhere', as it was known, has acquired
an almost mythical status, hard to appreciate unless you can
understand that curious cocktail of nostalgia, sentiment and
overwhelming sense of loss that fuels railway enthusiasm. It
was 'an extraordinary network of routes', writes Matthew Engel
in his book *Eleven Minutes Late,*

> stitched together in 1893 from a series of individual lines,
> and extending for 183 miles from its two separate junctions
> with the Great Northern north of Peterborough across the
> wide open spaces of the Fens and rural Norfolk. It was like
> a giant fantasy, with a map reminiscent of the Rev. W.
> Awdry's map of Sodor. The M & GN barely seemed to
> intersect with the real world; little golden-ochre engines
> pulled varnished wooden carriages to places an outsider
> might hardly believe existed.

When the entire M & GN network was shut by British Railways in 1959, except for the little stretch along the coast from here to West Runton, Sheringham and Melton Constable, it was the biggest single railway closure yet seen in Britain. Herein perhaps lies the paradox of the line's attraction: the more the memories fade, the greater the potency of the legend in the magical, misty-eyed and ultimately unreachable country of railway enthusiasm.

These days, to most people's eyes, Cromer station is a sad place – just a single platform with a bus shelter and a disused signal box. Where the sidings once stood and where the shiny blue Claud Hamilton express engines of the Great Eastern Railway were buffed and polished before the journey back to Liverpool Street stands a large Morrisons supermarket and a Carpetright warehouse designed in the modern fake vernacular style intended to be inoffensive but which is frequently quite the opposite. The splendid Arts and Crafts-style M & GN station building still stands, though it has become, according to the sign outside, BUDDIES BAR AND LOUNGE. NORTH NORFOLK'S PREMIER NIGHTCLUB. LIVE DJS. SKY SPORTS AND WEEKLY BANDS. At least the awning over what was once the ticket office entrance has been preserved, with the railway's initials still embedded ornately in the wrought iron. I ask a group of men, stripped to the waist and drinking bottles of Budweiser outside, accompanied by a ferocious-looking bull terrier, if the Midland and Great Northern Railway means anything to them. 'Dunno what you're talking about, mate. But if you're wanting a ticket, they ain't sold any here for years.'

I head for the exit, where there's a sign saying WELCOME TO CROMER, GEM OF THE NORFOLK COAST – and gem, if such a word has any meaning in the cliché book of tourism, it turns out to be. Not much seems to have changed since it was described in Jane Austen's *Emma* as 'the best of all sea bathing places'. The Crossways tobacconist on the road to the seafront has advertisements for 'Bishop's Move' tobacco and 'special medicated snuff' as well as a window full of politically incorrect paraphernalia. Especially prized here seem to be those revolving ashtrays once ubiquitous in every respectable British sitting room but these days only to be found in the bars of cheap Balkan hotels. Cromer recently had the blessing of John Betjeman's daughter Candida Lycett-Green, who wrote an article in the *Oldie* magazine in July 2010 extolling its virtues: 'Cromer is a magical place . . . all red-pantile roofs, cedar trees, pinnacled Edwardian houses with flamboyant verandahs' set against 'a broad back-drop of slate-blue sea'. She adds, 'It was the arrival of the railway in 1877 which finally put the gilt on Cromer's gingerbread . . .'

It certainly did, and by Edwardian times Cromer was among the most fashionable of seaside resorts. The new trains were filled with well-heeled holidaymakers who packed the swank hotels. But the glory did not last long. For decades Cromer slumbered in slightly shabby gentility, although these days it is being rediscovered by a different middle-class tribe, who are thronging the Waitrose and Marks & Spencer cookery demonstrations on the seafront this afternoon.

At least that grande dame of Edwardian hospitality, the Hotel de Paris, is still in business. Smart-jacketed waiters lounge at the entrance high above the pier, its wallflower-red sandstone frontage now heavily worn by more than a century of spray. Old ladies toddle in on walking sticks for afternoon tea as they have done for more than a century. Back then it was the seafront residence of Lord Suffield, and Edward VII would slip in by a side entrance for a spot of recreation with Lily Langtry. 'Stephen Fry was once a waiter here,' one woman tells me proudly. 'He looked lovely in his uniform, and was especially fond of old ladies! These days, there are so many old folk here, they call it the Saga Hotel.'

Could there be a jollier spring afternoon at the English seaside than today? Small boys jostle each other as they cast for crabs off the pier while the mayors of Cromer and Sheringham rattle their chains as they prepare to present awards for the most impressive catch. Tonight at the Pier Theatre Joe Brown 'of Joe Brown and the Bruvvers, the famous 1960s rock group' is playing. (Not so different, in their ability to thrill today's oldies, from Herr Moritz Wurm and the Blue Viennese Band, who topped the bill in Edwardian times.) On the seafront an elderly fisherman flashes arthritic fingers to weave a crab trap. 'Just call me Speedy,' he says. 'Doesn't half make your fingers sore when the wife asks you to do the washing up afterwards. But these Cromer crabs are the tastiest in the country. We catch 'em small, you see,' he tells me in a 'Singing Postman' Norfolk lilt. 'But they're stupid buggers – you can get forty or fifty of 'em crawling into the trap at the same time.'

As the sun starts to set and the ice-cream sellers pack up, the trains are few and far between, so I decide to walk along the coast to my destination for the night – the old Midland and Great Northern Railway's hotel at West Runton, the next station along the line to Sheringham. The M & GN may not have had much of a talent for running railways, but it spotted an opportunity to develop a coastline of fishing villages marooned in the Middle Ages into what it hoped would be a playground for its clients – the weary miners and hosiery workers of the east Midlands. Why would anyone want to build a rambling half-timbered Edwardian hotel in the middle of a north Norfolk village backwater? Answer: plan a golf course around it. And it is this that has helped what is now called the Links Country Park Hotel stagger into the twenty-first century, as the holiday camps and boarding houses around here have fallen out of fashion.

The walk, parallel to the tracks along a National Trust coast, starts promisingly, past sunny pastel beach huts. In some parts of north Norfolk beach huts sell to affluent Londoners for more than the price of a terraced house in areas of northern England. Seemingly endless caravan sites dominate the view. (What is the collective noun for a large number of caravans on a beautiful coastline? The London media folk who have colonised the nearby Georgian town of Holt might say 'excrescence', but who is to deny these neat caravanners their lovely views of the sun setting over the sea as they fire up their barbecues?)

I am hot and hungry when I book into the hotel, which sits next to the single-platform station. The Links is a grand and rather elegant dowager with make-up fading – the gilded o from the hotel name has fallen off the façade. It was while staying here, recovering from enteric fever, that Arthur Conan Doyle had the idea for his famous mystery *The Hound of the Baskervilles*, drawing on the ghostly legend of Black Shuck, the hell hound of Norfolk, who was said to have roamed the lanes along the coast. The ivy-clad Gothic façade of nearby Cromer Hall is supposed to have been the model for Baskerville Hall. How did the story get translated to Dartmoor? Who knows? But visible from my bedroom window is Beacon Hill, at 338 feet the highest point in Norfolk. No dramatic West Country moor, certainly, but dramatic enough and a rebuttal of the great myth about the county perpetuated by Noel Coward in his play *Private Lives*: 'Very flat, Norfolk.'

There's more drama still to be had in West Runton, as I head hungrily for the only pub in the village. I fantasise that 'choux puffs with Cromer crab and coriander' might be on the menu, as well as some other foodie marvels from the crab festival afternoon. 'No food tonight, mate,' says the young barman. 'But it was a bit different here in the old days,' he tells me as I settle for a packet of salt and vinegar crisps and half a pint of Adnam's. 'Can you believe the Sex Pistols played here once? And T. Rex, The Clash, the Boomtown Rats, King Crimson, Thin Lizzy, Blue Oyster Cult . . .' He reels off a fantasy line-up of rock bands from the 1970s. 'Before my time. You look as though you might remember them days, mate. Look at the blue plaque outside.' It turns out that this was the site of the legendary West Runton Pavilion, a dance hall converted to an off-the-beaten-track venue for groups to test out their UK tours. The idea was that the remoteness made it inaccessible to sneery metropolitan music journalists. Even Chuck Berry played here before the pavilion was demolished in 1986. But who will ever know whether the Father of Rock'n'Roll arrived on the tracks of the Midland and Great Northern or if this sleepy Norfolk village once reverberated to his famous song 'Downbound Train':

> The passengers were most a motley crew,
> Some were foreigners and others he knew.
> Rich men in broadcloth, beggars in rags,
> Handsome young ladies and wicked old hags.

Surely he cannot have been referring to the ladies of the West Runton and District Women's Institute, who are busy watering the station garden when I arrive to catch the early train to Sheringham next morning. Here are Jane Bothwell and her WI friends, who have adopted the station and turned the site of the demolished buildings into a kind of paradise garden – a riot of early summer bloom, with roses tumbling over a pergola. 'Look, this is a heuchera, and this a phormium,' she tells me. 'And this is a Margery Fish clematis.' 'Don't worry about me,' says one of the husbands helping out. 'I'm just an appendage and I do what I'm told.' The station noticeboard is festooned with certificates – 'Gold Award, Anglia in Bloom', 'Best Community Rail Image', 'Voted Best Station Adopter Group'. 'I've lived round here all my life and I've known this station since I was a girl,' says Mrs Bothwell. 'Here, where the geraniums are, was once the stationmaster's house. It used to be full of life and we keep the site alive to this day. We love this place.'

'You tangle with these ladies at your peril,' says Ian Dinmore, Norfolk County Council's community rail officer, who is aboard the train, busy on his beat, chivvying up the local communities to use and get involved with the line. 'They are the most ferocious protectors of the local railways. If Beeching ever came along here again, I wouldn't fancy his chances.' Ian, the son of a railwayman, who ended his British Railways career as one of the now extinct breed of East Anglian stationmasters, now treads the fine line between hard-headed commercial rail operators and communities determined never to have another Beeching closure again, even if most local people actually prefer their cars. But there can be no greater enthusiast than Ian, whose knowledge of the line is encyclopedic. 'Did you see the concrete pigs by the track up to Cromer? And some say that a headless horseman appears alongside the line at Gunton on the anniversary of Ann Boleyn's death?'

Ian is especially delighted about the recently reopened link between the Network Rail terminus at Sheringham and the five-mile rump of the M & GN line to Holt, severed nearly half a century ago by Beeching, which is now run by preservationists as the Poppy Line. The 200-yard track connection across a busy road means that trains can run directly onto one of Britain's most successful heritage railways. Why go to the trouble of severing it in the first place? British Railways managers had no interest in maintaining links with lines that they regarded as fit for the scrapheap, especially as they saw preservationists succeeding where they had failed. To this day there are thriving preserved lines possessing junctions with the national network across which trains are not allowed to run. Even on the new link at Sheringham Network Rail has imposed a limit of twelve trains a year.

On the other side of the crossing, in the old porters' office in the Poppy Line station, I have a cup of tea with Trevor Eady, the general manager. 'I'm not a rail buff or a railwayman,' he says. 'Until I retired I was a manager at Norwich airport.' But he seems to know a lot about the old railway and tells me proudly of how his thirty-two staff and 600 volunteers have captured the atmosphere of the old M & GN. 'The station here is painted in the authentic colours of the old railway company. After being cut back to almost nothing, how nice for the M & GN to be expanding again. But this is no mausoleum. People will always be interested in the railways. All you need is to have a steam loco sitting out in the platform and families suddenly appear from all over the place. For folk who have never seen a steam train – and there are more and more of them – it's a mystery and a marvel.'

'But what about the poppies on the Poppy line?' I ask since it occurs to me that I haven't seen a single one on my journey. 'Ah,' he says, slightly embarrassed. 'Well, we don't always mean it literally.'

Poppyland, apparently, was a name coined by Clement Scott, a Victorian theatre critic of the *Daily Telegraph*. For the world-weary journalist, north Norfolk was a land of dreams – especially as he appears to have installed a mistress locally – and Scott wrote a series of drippingly sentimental articles about the area called the *Poppyland Papers* – though, something of a snob, he later he came to regret his part in popularising the area for the masses.

Back at Norwich Thorpe station, the 17.30 service home to London is already at the platform in the charge of Class 90 electric express locomotive No. 90005 *Vice Admiral Lord Nelson*. While the Cambridge Express was a suburban train pretending to be a grand one, this is quite the opposite – a once-grand train fallen on humbler times. In the new world of HS2, TGV, ICE and other super-fast trains defined by acronyms, *Lord Nelson* and its carriages are a dinosaur among expresses. The 1980s-built loco is rusting and patched in places with mastic, while the moquette in the once-luxurious Mark III coaches is fading, the carriages showing few signs of their former glamorous life on the crack Anglo-Scottish expresses from Euston to Glasgow. The final indignity came in 2009, when the Norwich trains lost all their restaurant cars, Lowestoft kippers for breakfast and all. This was the last all-day restaurant service on any main line railway in Britain, ending a tradition going back to 1879. Before long, modern multiple units will take over, and the days of heroic express trains on Liverpool Street services will be at an end. As he stands at the buffers in Liverpool Street at the close of his journey, *Vice Admiral Lord Nelson* emits a muffled electronic sigh, as though he knows that an era is almost at its close.

Fit for a Duke: Originally the private station of the Dukes of Sutherland, Dunrobin Castle is one of the charms of the Far North Line for modern travellers. Here, a Class 158 unit arrives with an Inverness-bound train on 30 June 2010.

CHAPTER TWO

THE 10.38 TO THE FAR NORTH – THE TRAIN TO THE END OF THE WORLD

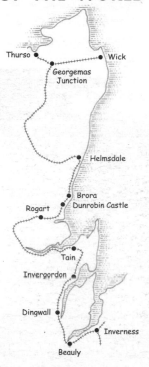

Inverness to Wick and Thurso, via Beauly, Dingwall, Invergordon, Tain, Rogart, Dunrobin Castle, Brora, Helmsdale and Georgemas Junction

There is probably no more delightful way of arriving at a stately home anywhere in Britain than to step off a train onto the platform at the little private station of the Duke of Sutherland opposite the gates of Dunrobin Castle, the grandest house in the Scottish Highlands. Fortunately we are privileged to do so thanks to the curious enthusiasms of George Granville William Sutherland Leveson-Gower, Viscount Trentham, Marquis of Stafford and third Duke of Sutherland.

Unlike most of his fellow aristocrats in the High Victorian era, the duke took neither the view that the railways were simply a way of harvesting a quick buck, nor did he sit back in his club and snort at the outrage of these newfangled inventions emitting smoke and noise near his country estates. George Granville was a prototype of the modern railway enthusiast – he loved the steamy monsters of his age so obsessively that he served as an apprentice in the sooty works of the London and North Western Railway at Wolverton because he wanted to understand how they worked. Then he built a railway to access his Dunrobin Castle estate, commissioning his own engine and train and ultimately his own private station a few steps from the gates of his castle in Sutherland. Which is where I am alighting from the Inverness to Wick train this afternoon.

Today the little station, built in the half-timbered style of the rest of the estate, is as tranquil as the day when the duke drove the royal train containing Queen Victoria and her retinue almost to his front door. The original *Dunrobin* locomotive has long since gone to the scrapyard, but you can still feel quite lordly stepping onto the platform to stride past the charabanc crowds in the car park to enter this magnificent Gothic pile. And unlike the motorists who have jousted with the traffic on the A9 to get here, thanks to the vision of the railway enthusiast duke, we have been privileged to arrive via one of the most dramatic and scenic railway lines in Britain.

The Far North Line, into which the duke's railway was eventually merged, takes us on a 180-mile journey from Inverness to Wick and Thurso – the most northerly town in Britain – along a meandering route linking beaches, firths, sea and freshwater lochs and remote moorland rivers. The single-track railway passes small harbours, tall mountains and wild and eerie moorland punctuated by isolated villages. It passes through the dramatic Flow Country, one of the richest wildernesses in northern Europe. It takes a leisurely route along the shores of three firths at Beauly, Dornoch and Cromarty, and hugs the banks of the Helmsdale River, rich in salmon and gold – literally, since it was the scene of an unlikely gold rush in 1868, and optimistic folk still pan the river for gold today.

For lovers of curiosities the line boasts four unique features on the national rail network. It has the smallest station in Scotland at Beauly, the most isolated at Altnabreac, the most northerly railway junction in the UK at Georgemas Junction and the shortest distance between two stations on a main line – Culrain and Invershin Halt. The railway also serves as a living timeline of the social history of the north of Scotland: the fallout from the Highland Clearances, the rise and decline of the herring industry, the threat from Beeching in the 1960s, who wanted to close every bit of track north of the Caledonian Canal, the North Sea oil boom and the recent renaissance of high-tech Inverness, which claims to be the fastest-growing city in Europe. When Paul Theroux travelled to Wick for his book *The Kingdom by the Sea* back in 1983, he described the line as 'doomed' and 'on its last legs'. Thankfully it is still with us and flourishing as never before, though, like the way in which the tracks cling to loch, seashore and hillside, its existence is ever likely to be precarious.

I had set off from Euston the night before on the Inverness portion of the 21.15 Highland Sleeper, a train which always evokes a wistful sense of glamour as though it knows it is one of the last truly romantic trains on the British national network and may not survive as such for ever. There's already a whiff of the Highlands on board, with haggis, neeps and tatties, and barley soup on the menu in the lounge car. I settle for a bottle of Traquair House Ale produced at the stately home of the same name. It seems appropriate for getting in the mood, since the label recounts how the gates of Traquair were closed after a visit from Bonnie Prince Charlie, and the Earl of

Traquair vowed they would never be opened again until a Stuart king was crowned in London. The train is said to have more aristocratic regulars than any other in Britain. What about the old sandy-whiskered chap across the vestibule, who knocked back three glasses of Tomatin single malt before Watford? Could he be a laird on the way back to the ancestral estate? I shall never find out, since he is already dozing off.

After a journey of nearly twelve hours as far north as it is possible to travel on a single train from London I am having breakfast in the grand dining room of the Royal Highland Hotel in Inverness. 'We used to be known as the Station Hotel,' the waitress confides. 'But anything called a station hotel sounds a wee bit, well, cheap these days, doesn't it?' (The Royal Highland might want to play down another aspect of its heritage – the stairway on which I'm standing was the model for the grand stairway on the *Titanic*.) There's still some time before the departure of my northbound train to walk round to the freight yard to see the arrival of the 'Tesco Express' – the daily container train that overturns the wisdom that supermarket deliveries are most efficiently done by heavy lorries. Even more bizarrely, the train is operated by that king of the road Eddie Stobart, and the wagons even bear his corporate logo. Eddie Stobart trains? Whatever next? 'Did you know that Inverness and its surrounds are the most "Tescofied" area of Britain?' says the man on the gate, who lets me sneak in to watch as the wagons are unloaded for local distribution. 'Here the locals say yes to Tesco, it's the middle-class incomers who moan about them.'

But no time for chit-chat, as I can already see my 10.38 departure to the far north heading into the platform. Hurrah, it's a Class 158 diesel multiple unit that looks as though it's just emerged from the carriage washer. You don't need to be a train buff to enjoy the slow trains of Britain nor to have underlined a number in a spotter's book to enjoy what they offer, but it is handy to know which lines have better trains.

This is one of them – newly refurbished, clean and with low windows that line up with the seats, a feature universal in British trains until the 1960s, but now such a rarity that one must assume that every modern train builder appoints an engineer whose sole job is to think up ideas to annoy the passenger. We may also feel a little smug, since the neighbouring West Highland Line, which is always boasting about the superiority of its scenery, is operated by far less comfortable Class 156 trains.

The 10.38 pulls over the junction with the line to Aberdeen and past the stone buildings of the Lochgorm Works, where the handsome steam locomotives of the old Highland Railway were once built and where modern trains like ours are still maintained. The Highland may have been a minnow among railways, but its engineers William Stroudley and David Jones produced some of the most elegantly proportioned engines ever built, decked out in pea-green and mustard-yellow. One of the finest – the Jones Goods 4-6-0 – can be seen in the Glasgow Museum of Transport. Soon we are crossing one of the few operational railway swing bridges left on the rail network, over Telford's great Caledonian Canal past the little wooden signal box at Clachnaharry, itself the last operative box on the line, since all other signalmen on the line have been done away with.

The saviour of the line has been the modern Radio Electronic Token Block system operated from a control centre at Inverness, which has allowed staff to be reduced to a handful. First stop is Beauly, as beautiful as the literal meaning of its name. It was closed in 1960 but reopened in 2002 as part of an initiative to get Inverness commuters onto the rails. Cash was so tight that only a tiny bleak platform could be afforded and passengers queue to enter just one door of the train. It is the local station of Ann Gloag, who with her brother Brian Souter founded the Stagecoach rail and bus group, and owns nearby Beaufort Castle. Has the richest and most powerful woman in the entire history of the railways ever stepped aboard a train here? Nobody I speak to has ever heard of such a thing. At the next stop, Muir of Ord, passengers once changed for the Black Isle Line to Fortrose. (The Black Isle is not an isle but a peninsula, and not as sinister as it sounds). The line was shut in 1960, before it even had a chance to become a glimmer in Beeching's eye.

Could there be a more complete country junction – especially in a place so remote – than Dingwall, the next station? Here the line splits, turning off to the west to Kyle of Lochalsh and the Isle of Skye – the 'iron road to the isles'. The handsome station buildings in pink sandstone with a delicate and airy glass canopy are still in use and contain a staffed ticket office, a station pub called the Mallard and a tearoom where there is a plaque proclaiming that 134,864 servicemen were given cups of tea here during the First World War. The station also, somewhat surrealistically, incorporates a Christian bookshop. Could this too be due to the influence of Mrs Gloag, who is a well-known Presbyterian? Certainly everything at Dingwall is in place for the nourishment of body and soul.

Before setting off from here, the driver has to get out of his cab to press a plunger to set the points for where the line diverges for Kyle of Lochalsh. As he does so, an elderly man hobbling with a stick brandishes a jug of milk. 'He's a local farmer and has offered refreshment to all the crews since time immemorial,' I'm told. The gaunt-looking tower on the hill above the station is a memorial to Sir Hector MacDonald – 'Fighting Mac' as he was known – one of the most famous Victorian generals. Accused of homosexuality while commander of British armed forces in Ceylon, he shot himself in a Paris hotel. Was Sir Hector the model for the iconic kilted soldier on the Camp Coffee bottle? There are many who think so – and the unfortunate kilted Sir Hector may have played his part in coining the modern usage of the word 'camp'.

The train is now picking up speed, crossing over the Dingwall Canal, Britain's most northerly inland waterway, and along the shore of Cromarty Firth. Here are the first signs of 'black gold' – in the form of skeletal hulks of oil rigs berthed for repair in the deep waters. 'You'll find it a lot more scenic as we get further north,' says Kenny, the conductor. 'My favourite stretch of the line is where we run along the seashore – you'll see seals galore there.' A lot of chatter and a buzzy community atmosphere in the carriage develops as the train fills up along the way. Like rural slow trains across the land, the journey reflects the rich social fabric of the region. Here's a bunch of ladies off to do their shopping, passing the time of day with the manager of an organic salmon farm. ('They supply Waitrose, you know,' one of them tells me in an awed hush.) A couple of lithe Lycra-clad cyclists are anxiously guarding their sleek hand-built Condor machines, which they have suspended from the bike rack. They are off to do the John o'Groats to Land's End cycle run. This is the third time they've completed it, apparently. 'But stay clear of John o'Groats itself,' they tell me. 'It's a theme park and a dump.'

At Alness I get chatting to Stewart Campbell, a quietly spoken semi-retired GP who has ministered to the sick of this remote area for a quarter of a century. 'These days I look after the flower beds at Alness station and take the train regularly along the line to Helmsdale, where I still work one day a week. It's a real lifeline, this railway,' he tells me, settling down to educate me about its history. How it was built in stages from 1862 and opened all the way to Wick in 1874 with forty-five stations along the way. 'In those days there were only two trains a day, which were so slow that it was impossible to get to the end of the line and back in the hours of daylight for most of the year.' It continued almost unscathed until 1960, when a pre-Beeching cull closed many of the small wayside halts. Then came the prospect of Armageddon as Beeching included the line in his slash-and-burn policy north of Inverness. But it survived and, now shielded by the pro-rail Scottish government, is as safe as it has ever been, with four trains a day including a Sunday service, as well as an even more frequent commuter service at the southern end into the Highland capital.

You can't miss Invergordon – the disused station buildings are rendered cheerful with *trompe l'oueil* murals, including a ticket clerk peering cheekily out of a booking office window, and at Tain the famous distillery can be seen alongside the line. This is notable for having the tallest stills in Scotland and for producing its popular Glenmorangie whisky from hard rather than soft water. But it is a long time since the raw materials were brought here or to any of the other distilleries along the line by train. Fortunately there is some of the finished product on board, and this might be the time to order a dram or two from the refreshment trolley, for we are about to undertake an almighty diversion which will force us to lag far behind the motorists on the parallel A9 road.

The line from Inverness to Wick does not follow a direct route, since the heavily indented coastline is not designed for easy communication. A reasonably direct route would have been challenging to Victorian engineers and cost more than the original investors – even the 'Railway Duke' – were prepared to support. Writing in 1952 in his book *Lines of Character,* the engineer L T C Rolt put it like this:

At Tain, where our train met the southern shore of
Dornoch Firth we were but five miles by crow-flight from
Dornoch, capital of Sutherland and the smallest county
town in Scotland if not in all of Britain. Yet to reach
Dornoch by rail we had still to cover no less than 44
miles. In its early days, the Great Western Railway was
sometimes facetiously described as the Great Way Round
but its most devious route was direct compared with the
example of the Highland.

The chance for the railway to remedy this was lost in 1991, when the North Sea oil boom led to the building of a new bridge to carry the road over the firth. Somehow the money could not be found to include the railway track on the bridge too. But look what we would have missed. Over the waters and on the shore can be spied grey heron, shelduck, oyster-catcher and redshank. In the winter there are pink-footed geese, widgeon and teal, not to mention Atlantic salmon and trout seduced by the clear waters of the firth. The trolley lady, who has been patiently pushing her charge up and down the train since we left Inverness and will do so until we get to Wick, is unfazed by the time the journey takes. Although her blue eyes and dark hair give her a more Celtic appear-ance than almost anyone in the carriage, she is in fact Polish and tells me she is called Agnieszka. 'I came here four years ago and started work in Butlins in – how you say it – Bognor Regis?' She pulls a face as though she has stepped in some-thing unpleasant. 'But here I feel happy on this train, and I never tire of these lovely landscapes. I spoke no English when I came here and now I speak fluent Scottish. And I have even been as far as Edinburgh and Glasgow . . .'

But Agnieszka has to move on to serve some more drams as the line turns back on itself at the head of the firth on its long diversion round the shore. We pass Carbisdale Castle, a folly built by the second wife of the Duke of Sutherland after his family spurned her on his death. It is now a youth hostel. The clock on the tower has only three faces – the one facing towards Dunrobin is blank because she 'wouldn't give the Sutherlands the time of day'. It takes but a trice to get over the wrought iron Oykel Viaduct from Culrain to Inver-shin Halt, the shortest journey between two stations in Britain, although fans of the London Tube might claim that Covent Garden to Leicester Square is shorter. I buy a ticket as a souvenir, even though I have already paid for the journey. Judging from the look on Kenny's face I realise that he has quietly written me off as a barking eccentric. It turns out the rules of the railway would have also allowed me to have made a seat reservation. Wish I'd done that too.

We're heading back to the coast now past Lairg, with its little siding for the weekly oil train. This is the farthest north that the freight trains come these days, a far cry from the days when the consignment of goods and chattels was the main function of the line. Back in 1963 John Chamney was a BR clerk tasked with analysing the flow of goods on the 6.40 a.m. train from Inverness, which at that time included parcel vans. He reckoned the revenue from parcels was about seven times that of passengers. In his manifest he found compressor parts from Camborne in Cornwall to Thurso, a crate from the Ministry of Defence at Devonport for Invergordon, a Bush Radio from Plymouth to Brora, a stool from Frome to Bonar Bridge, marine equipment from Henley-on-Thames to Wick, a Parker Knoll chair by mail order from High Wycombe to Dornoch, as well as two boxes of Swiss rolls from Birmingham to Brora and two boxes of Tilley's crumpets from Cheltenham to Invergordon.

After passing the site of The Mound station, scene of much mourning when the Dornoch branch, operated uniquely by GWR pannier tanks, closed in 1960, I tip Kenny off that I want to alight at Dunrobin, which is a request stop and open in the summer months only. The guidebooks describe Dunrobin Castle, mostly fashioned in Victorian Gothic style by Sir Charles Barry, designer of the Houses of Parliament, as like something out of a fairy tale. But as the mists swirl around the towers off the North Sea on this chilly after-noon, it seems more akin to Tolkien's tower of Minas Morgul, an impression not dispelled by its gloomy entrance with stags' heads and tartan everywhere. But there are small treas-ures to be discovered. In the library, its floor covered with terrifying lion- and tiger-skin rugs, is a poignant portrait of the third duke as a ten-year-old, drawn by his sister, with a caption explaining how the young boy was fascinated by 'machines and locomotives'. Imagine – without one small boy and his hobby there might never have been a railway here at all.

The last trains on the Far North Line come early, and I have to rush to flag down the 18.01 back south to Rogart, where I am to break my journey, staying for the second night running in a sleeping car, though this one is destined not to turn a wheel. The carriage belongs to Frank Roach and his wife Kate, who live in the old stone station buildings with their three children and rent out three carriages as accommodation in a B & B business they call Sleeperzzz. Everybody around here knows Frank, who is king of the Far North Line, as well as its cheerleader-in-chief and business manager. In his role as partnership manager of the Highlands and Islands Regional Transport Partnership, he keeps the bosses of ScotRail on their toes and drums up new business for the line. But he is an old-school rail fan too, as evinced by the jumble of old station signs and railwayana around the platform. He has even acquired a former signal box, which he uses to grow tomatoes.

'I'd always fancied living in a railway station,' Frank tells me in his family's crowded kitchen, which was once the station booking office. 'My father was vicar of St Michael's Mount in Cornwall, and there was a great view of the famous Pullman camping coaches at Marazion. I guess the idea of this place entered my consciousness subliminally. As a child we used to go everywhere by train. Trains were my way out.'

Kate chips in: 'I knew Frank was keen on trains, though I'm not to the same degree But it's been an idyllic place to bring up our children, though it's hard work running the accommodation business. As well as the coaches, we've got an old Highland bus that people like to stay in, and we've got a couple in our old fairground coach tonight – they chose it for the double bed. Well, they're young . . .'

'What's nice about this place,' Frank says, 'is it's not full of second homes. We don't pander to tourism round here. I've seen west Cornwall ruined.' He pours some large slugs of Glenmorangie as the evening grows dark. 'This line is an undiscovered jewel. But the real appeal is it's so far away – beyond the clutches of corporate Britain. Our old friends from down south come here once and don't come back. It's too much of a whack. Four hours from Inverness to Wick – it's not for the faint-hearted. But it helps you slow down.'

'Yes,' says Kate, 'it gives you time to talk to people. We'll never leave. I tell you, we'll be out of here in boxes.'

Tonight I am on a train between Waterloo and Exeter in the 1970s, lying in bed in a compartment of a British Railways Mark II carriage. But it's not just in my dreams. I know it's real because I recognise the blue moquette on the seats and the Network Southeast colours in the door well. There are authentic Edward Pond murals under the luggage rack, whose bland design must have dispatched many a commuter into the land of Nod after a heavy day at the office. Is that the sound of a Class 50 thundering up Honiton bank? or is it the microwave in the kitchen along the corridor? No matter. Kate and Frank have fitted my bunk out so commodiously that I sleep soundly till morning.

'Ye'll nay find a better stretch of coastal railway in Britain,' says Keith the conductor aboard the early train north next morning, as the train approaches Brora. This is a claim I've heard in other parts, but Keith has a theory. 'You know why they talk up that bit of coast in Devon around Dawlish? Because most Englishmen can't be arsed to make the journey up here.' This is a rough, wild coast where waves froth on black rocks and fat seals take a breather a few yards from the tracks. It is as dramatic as any railway journey I have ever taken.

Maybe Keith is right about the unadventurous English, as I am the only passenger to alight at Helmsdale, an old-fashioned north-east-of-Scotland fishing village, beautiful in a harsh kind of way. On the track down to the station I spot a trendy-looking museum called timespan (four pounds to get in – a hefty charge in a part of Scotland without much work and where pay is low). The lower-case title gives it away, and my suspicions are confirmed when I am invited to step into the virtual 'Helmsdale history street'. Why bother, when there seems to be plenty of the real stuff about? In the old harbour, built by Thomas Telford, there's not much going on except some fishermen mending their nets aboard an ancient trawler and a couple of teals busy building a nest. 'The herring's all gone,' one of the fishermen tells me. 'It was once our silver. And the fish were a kind of silver that never needed to be polished. There was gold too, up at Kildonan – as well as the stuff that flowed out of the distilleries. But they're all owned by foreign firms now. As for the fish, these days the entire catch can be transported in a couple of white vans.'

But there are still lobster pots in the front gardens of the little houses along the harbour front. Pebbledash dour, they are as far from picture-postcard St Ives as can be. No self-respecting Cornish village would tolerate the scrapyard where the Helmsdale River flows out to sea. In the Belgrave Arms Hotel tonight it is still possible to get that old fashioned Scots staple a 'small fish tea' in the public bar. But the newer world of urban downshifters is creeping in. Just up from the post office is the Twentieth Century Collectibles shop, and the Mirage Café boasts that Clarissa Dickson Wright has nominated it one of Britain's 'top six fish and chip shops', though I'm not sure what this says about waistlines in the area, which are already generous.

At the station the mood is pure *Marie Celeste*. The old signal box is still there on the platform just as it was when the signalman pulled the last lever and hung up his duster. The handsome old Highland Railway station building is boarded up but without a single daub of graffiti. The housing for the station clock on the wall is there just as it was on the day the spring was finally wound. 'Probably sold it in some fancy Edinburgh auction house,' says the only other passenger, a retired fisherman off to visit his son in Thurso. He lights up a cigarette. 'Yes, it's allowed north of the border. Not like on station platforms in England. There's some English chappie who's put in a bid for the station. Rather leave it as it is than have that kind of thing here.'

Travelling north again, the train follows the course of the Helmsdale River – slate-grey and glassy in a muted green valley, and the land gets progressively bleaker and flatter as we enter the low country beyond the Highlands. At Kildonan station bling-seekers might get off for a bit of panning in the local burns. Back in 1869 hundreds flocked here Klondike-style after newspaper reports that there was 'gold in them thar hills'. Nobody ever managed to find much – though you never know. The Sutherland estates will still grant you a permit to go panning today.

The train is now more than three hours out of Inverness and slumbering passengers suddenly waking might be forgiven for thinking they were on the Trans-Siberian as the trees disappear to be replaced by vast tracts of black bog. Paul Theroux described it as something 'straight out of *Dracula* or the *Mountains of Madness*', a 'strange and forbidding wilderness' of black lochs, lonely moor and dark bogs. The most prominent features on the landscape are frequent vertical stumps by the trackside, which look like Neolithic objects of worship but are, more mundanely, railway sleepers designed to stop snow being swept onto the tracks. They are so rotten that they cannot be of much use. Or perhaps the 'wrong kind of snow' no longer settles in the far north of Scotland?

This melancholy landscape is the Flow Country, a vast tract of spongy moss adorned as far as the eye can see by white bog cotton. Easy to imagine that if you stepped off here, it could swallow you instantly with a watery gulp. But you are not alone. Here are rare short-eared owls and hen harriers, and if you look hard you might spot a merlin swooping on its prey.

The train is climbing and the engine grinding hard now on the 1-in-60 gradient to County March summit, before reaching Altnabreac, the loneliest station on the line and perhaps in the whole of Britain. No road, just a couple of houses and a hostel for walkers. But it had its charms for the novelist Lisa St Aubin de Terán, who wrote her book *Off the Rails: Confessions of a Train Addict* while living in one of the houses here. There are other unusual distinctions too. During the two world wars twenty-coach troop trains would come this way from Euston on their way to Thurso and on to Scapa Flow, the Royal Navy's base in the Orkneys. The twenty-two-hour, 717-mile journey might have seemed like a prison sentence to the troops on board, but the trains were literally a jail for prisoners of war, who were carried in specially constructed cells aboard the carriages.

At Georgemas Junction I run into Mike Lunan, former convener of the Friends of the Far North Line, the passenger group that has worked hard to defeat threats of closure over the years. Mike used to be a financial adviser ('Folk round here are canny with their money, and I was the only one of the species'); these days he sets crosswords. 'I spend my days doing them as well, but sometimes they are too easy and don't fill the time. It's a bit like going to Lord's expecting to play a Test match and ending up against the village team.' Mike also bats against anyone who dares to threaten his beloved Far North Line. He's off to Argos in Wick today to do his shopping. 'Why use the car? We've got to look after our train service.'

But first the train has to go to Thurso, before reversing back down the line to Wick, travelling through Georgemas Junction twice. Once the carriages would split at Georgemas and separate engines took the portions in opposite directions. But that became too costly, so the present arrangement was adopted, adding ten miles to the journey. But this complicated shuffle is marvellous news for Georgemas Junction, which at periods in the day has four trains in the space of an hour – the Clapham Junction of Caithness.

At Wick the original station with its wooden overall roof survives, adorned with a mural of an old David Jones 4-4-0 named *Caithness*, built by Dubs and Co. of Glasgow in 1874 and a reminder of the days when the trains were more elegant but slower and less comfortable than today. Not much time to hang around in Wick – we're due in at 2.55 but arrive ten minutes late, and soon it will be time for the last train south at 4.p.m – but there's something glamorous about getting to the extremity of any railway line. Think of Paddington to Penzance or even Finchley to Morden on the Northern Line (Britain's longest tunnel). As if to mark the achievement of getting this far there's a list of DISTINGUISHED VISITORS TO WICK inscribed on a granite stone on the station approach. Gladstone, Lloyd George, Ernest Shackleton and Robert Louis Stevenson came here in the good old days when the town was the herring capital of Britain. But today there's not even a scent of a herring to be had on the quayside.

At the height of Wick's fishing boom there were 6,000 fishermen, the town boasted forty-five pubs to service their thirst, and on a typical day 700 bottles of whisky might be drunk. I learn this from the barman in one of the surviving pubs, the Alexander Bain, named after the inventor of the electric clock and one of the town's most famous sons. Presumably Bain managed to stay off the hard stuff, since he is credited with also inventing the first facsimile machine and one of the earliest versions of the railway telegraph, which he installed along the line from Glasgow to Edinburgh.

I see Mike back at the station, clutching his shopping. 'What you've got to remember about this railway,' he tells me as we climb aboard the train, 'is that we are truly at the end of the line. There's nothing north of here. It's the end of the world so far as the British rail system goes. And to get here you've really got to want to come. There are plenty of rewards, though. Where else in the UK, for instance, do you get seventeen hours of daylight on a day like today?'

He waves goodbye at Georgemas Junction and, as if summoned by magic, the sun has returned, throwing into relief the weeds on the scarcely used platform like hairs on the back of a gnarled hand. The slowly setting sun continues to illuminate my four-hour-and-ten-minute journey back from the 'end of the world' to Inverness, where I change onto the Caledonian Sleeper for the long journey back to London. Darkness falls and I settle into my bunk as the train speeds south past Perth, on through the Lowlands towards Carlisle and Euston. I imagine Mike still on his veranda, the northerly sun not yet below the horizon, tussling with the toughest of crosswords and musing on ways to thwart the bureaucrats if ever his precious line to the end of the world should be threatened again.

The final whistle: Members of the Liskeard Drama Group perform the last rites for steam on the Liskeard to Looe branch, which ended on 10 September 1961. But a steam train returned nearly half a century later to celebrate the line's 150th anniversary in autumn 2010.

CHAPTER THREE

THE 16.40 FROM LISKEARD – BRITAIN'S MOST ECCENTRIC BRANCH LINE CELEBRATES ITS BIRTHDAY

Liskeard to Looe, via Coombe Junction Halt, St Keyne WishingWell Halt, Causeland and Sandplace

Even by the standards of London's opulent Grosvenor House Hotel, there can rarely have been a grander do than the banquet given to celebrate the centenary of the Great Western Railway in October 1935. And why shouldn't there have been the most splendid of parties? The company's directors, in that golden age of trains, had no reason not to believe in their own publicity – that the initials GWR really did stand for God's Wonderful Railway. More than 1,100 guests attended, including the Prince of Wales and the mayors and lord mayors of nearly every town and city served by the company. After the meal, which included fillet of sole and caviar, the prince gave a witty speech reminding guests that his great-grandmother Queen Victoria had first travelled by train on the GWR in 1842. His Royal Highness concluded that on the company's birthday it 'was entitled to have its trumpet blown and I am very happy to give it a hearty and resounding blast'.

Today, exactly three quarters of a century on, I'm off to join the official commemoration of the GWR's 175th – not with a 'blast' or a grand metropolitan nosh-up, but at a celebration on an obscure little branch line in one of the remotest corners of the land. Back in 1935 the Liskeard to Looe line would have been a pinprick on the map of a vast empire of brown-shaded lines extending from Paddington to Penzance and Birkenhead to Bodmin, and in 1966 it was deemed unworthy to survive when the closure notices went up. But survive it did, and today the modern-day directors of First Great Western, who now operate Brunel's great enterprise, have chosen to spare the caviar and spend the energy on helping to return a steam locomotive to the branch for the first time in fifty years. The grandees up at Paddington have noticed too that it also happens to be 150 years since the first trains ran along the brand new railway to Looe.

Running tortuously for just over eight miles, hugging the sides of an intimate wooded valley, there can be few branch lines in the world as idyllic as this one. First we are cloistered in the secret world of the valley; then, as the line approaches Looe, the trackbed is lapped by the tranquil waters of the East Looe River estuary. Here are ancient trees dipping their boughs in the water and on the reeded flats you can spy oystercatchers, curlews and egrets. In the woods lurk jays, greater spotted woodpeckers and nuthatches. You may be lucky, as you look out of the window towards the river, to see a flash of blue – the unmistakable sign of a kingfisher. But the line is also a treasure trove of oddities and curiosities – trains that travel in the wrong direction, a haunted station, a junction paradoxical in its name since you can't change trains there, and which has one of the tiniest numbers of users on the network. Here also are Britain's last two stations on the national network with the official designation 'halt'. The Looe line, appropriately, is also famous for one of the most unusual railway loos in Britain – of which more later.

Arriving at Liskeard from the London train to change onto the Looe branch, passengers find themselves almost immediately in the topsy-turvy world of Lewis Carroll's *Through the Looking-Glass and What Alice Found There*. 'All this time the guard was looking at her, first through a telescope and then through a microscope, and then through an opera-glass. At last, he said, "You're travelling the wrong way," and shut up the window and went away. "So young a child," said the gentleman sitting opposite her (he was dressed in white paper), "ought to know which way she's going, even if she doesn't know her own name."'

Today passengers changing trains at Liskeard find themselves as perplexed as Alice, since the platforms for the Looe branch are at right angles to the main line facing north, when the direction they expect to be travelling is south. Oh dear! More baffling still, the signs on the platform are all in the retro brown and cream enamel of the early British Railways era of the 1950s. Are we in some kind of time warp and dreaming, like Alice? But all is explained in a notice underneath the Victorian wooden canopy over the platform, where the decidedly contemporary Class 153 single-unit railcar is waiting impatiently to depart on the 16.14 down the valley.

Once upon a time, we learn, this was a not a railway at all, but a canal which carried rich supplies of granite and copper from Bodmin Moor. In 1860 the canal was supplemented by the newfangled Liskeard and Looe Railway, which joined with the Liskeard and Carodon Railway bringing minerals down from the hills to the north. But there was a problem. There was no connection to the London to Penzance main line – the closest station was at Coombe, way down in the vertiginous valley below – and it was too far to lug a suitcase along the steep lanes to the main line station at Liskeard. So in 1901 a Looe engineer called Joseph Thomas came up with an ingenious solution – a long and winding horseshoe curve under the main line, which ran on the viaduct 147 feet above, eventually coming into dock at right angles on the other side of the tracks. It is down this curvaceous 1 in 40 gradient that our single-coach train is heading precariously now, sensibly cautious since six carriages ran away here in 1906. But there's another obstacle to negotiate. By the time we have edged our way round the circuit to the valley floor, our train is facing north again. So we must reverse before our journey to the coast gets properly under way. In a well-rehearsed ritual, the driver changes ends; the conductor picks up the ancient metal token that will allow us to pass on our way and pulls the lever to change the points. In pre-railcar days, drivers found this particularly bothersome, since they had to shunt their locomotive round the train as well.

Lonely little Coombe Junction Halt is still there, tantalisingly in sight along the branch north of us. But these days only two trains a day are scheduled to pull into the platform, placing it in the record books as one of the least used stations in Britain. According to the latest statistics, fewer than one passenger a day joins or leaves a train here. Lonelier still is the line beyond Coombe, where rusting rails survive for the once-weekly goods train to a cement works at Moorswater. It was here, until the end of steam in 1961, that the most bizarre lavatory in Britain could be found, tucked behind the engine sheds. It comprised the firebox of the locomotive *Caradon* placed over a small tributary of (appropriately) the East Looe River. It gave a new meaning to the term *gardez l'eau,* which in medieval times had been shouted from bedroom windows as chamber pots were emptied into the street below. This is the origin of the modern euphemism 'loo' – though the word's increased popularity in recent years has been bad news, of course, for the image of the poor old town of Looe.

Heading south in the opposite direction, the line is hugged by a blanket of trees, though there are tantalising glimpses of the river and high grassy hills when the boughs are stirred by the breeze. There are still signs of the old canal, with tumbledown bridges and the mouldering remains of wooden lock gates. The rich, peaty and smoky smell of woodland in autumn drifts in through the windows, overlaid with a hint of wild garlic. You will have to alert the guard (though now you must call him in officialspeak 'train manager') if you wish to get off at the next station. This is the delightfully named St Keyne Wishing Well Halt, the other of the last two stations on the network officially designated 'halt'. The 'wishing well' is a few minutes' walk up the hill and derives its fame from a quirky story by the poet Robert Southey (1774–1843) about St Keyne, a fifth-century holy woman who imparted magical powers to the waters whereby 'whichever of a married couple should drink of them first, he or she would have mastery of their wedded life'. The Victorians loved such sentimental claptrap, and newly wed beauties would leap from the train and run up the steep hill in a desperate race with their husbands to gain household supremacy. Modern visitors are more likely to be attracted by a fantastical museum of old music machines, including cinema organs, Belgian fair organs, mighty Wurlitzers and pianolas, all housed in an old watermill next to the station. It was shut when I went, so I still don't know if any of them play 'Here Comes the Bride'.

Best not to linger too long at the next stop, Causeland, unless you are a ghost hunter, since the tiny platform here is reputedly one of the most haunted in Britain. (Liskeard station itself is said to have been the setting for the 1941 supernatural comedy thriller *The Ghost Train*, starring Arthur

Askey.) Legend has it that in her haste to be first from the train to dash up to the shrine at St Keyne, a young bride fell onto the track, breaking her neck. Since then there have been stories of a young woman in a wedding dress seen walking the line between Causeland and St Keyne. Fanciful perhaps, but there is a creepier and more modern legend. Visible from the train, inside the station shelter is a payphone, but not any old payphone. Reputedly, it is one of the busiest BT public telephones in the country for incoming calls. Strange for a phone that accepts only cards and is located in one of the most isolated parts of the kingdom. There are those who tell the tale of it ringing out day and night, but when it is answered there is only the sound of tapping at the end of the line . . .

Sandplace is another lonely station, with not a soul requesting a stop and no one on the platform to wave down the train. With no tickets to inspect, Dave the guard (oops, train manager) has time to tell me a yarn about a Chinese passenger who boarded a train at Bristol and had his ticket checked here. 'He'd asked for Crewe, but they sold him a ticket for Looe. He'd apparently pronounced it "Clooe" and they thought he meant Looe. But they sorted him out with another ticket and sent him on his way back to Plymouth, making sure he was looked after.'

I don't know whether to believe this any more than the tale of the phantom bride, but there's no time to speculate since the estuary is broadening out and suddenly there is a glorious vista across the sparkling blue water, where egrets and other aquatic birds bob around amid small white boats. This is the distillation of a perfect country branch line as described by Paul Theroux:

> There is an English dream of a warm summer evening on a branch line train. Just that sentence can make an English person over 40 fall silent with the memory of what has

become a golden fantasy of an idealised England: the comfortable dusty coaches rolling through the low woods, the sun gilding the green leaves and striking through the carriage windows; the breeze tickling the hot flowers in the fields, birdsong and the thump of a powerful locomotive; the pleasant creak of the wood panelling on the coach; the mingled smells of fresh grass and coal smoke . . .

All very well, you might say, so where's the steam engine? Well, one will be along tomorrow, pulling four special trains up and down the line on its special double birthday – 175 years of the mighty Great Western and 150 years of the little branch to Looe. As we nudge up to the buffers at Looe's tiny single platform, I think of how close we got to losing it. Beeching saw no use for the line and notices were posted for its complete closure in October 1966, but Transport Minister Barbara Castle reprieved it at the very last minute. She cited difficulties with access over the local roads as the reason for her decision, but there is the intriguing possibility that another factor swayed her – which I discovered recently in a fading newspaper cutting from the *Cornish Times*. One night back in 1945 a young man and his father walked along the track to the signal box at Liskeard to chat with the signalman, one Jack Pitts, Labour candidate for Bodmin in the general election. The young man was Harold Wilson – the future prime minister – and the signalman was reading a work by G D H Cole, the great socialist thinker. After a long discussion about the book, the young man signed on the dotted line and pledged to join the Labour Party. The rest is history. Could it be that a sentimental PM remembered that night and leant on his minister to save the railway that had helped set him on his path to fame?

Not much left of Looe station now – once the train has departed for Liskeard the place has a mournful and shuttered air – but down the twisty backstreets, amid some dusty rocks, old bones, parchments and other bric-a-brac in the little museum of Looe, housed in a former jail, can be found a model of the station as it was in the 1950s. Here were the sidings where china clay and granite were humped off a wagon into a 'dirty British coaster with a salt-caked smoke stack', in the words of Poet Laureate John Masefield, and crates of silvery fish were hauled off trawlers into insulated railway vans to be sped off, still exuding the salty tang of the sea, to the towns and cities of England.

All along the quayside of East Looe on this fine evening small boys dangle mackerel heads in the water, filling buckets to the brim with wriggling black crabs. I follow the line of where the tracks once ran to the end of the breakwater – the Banjo Pier – another masterpiece of civil engineering from Joseph Thomas, the man who built the horseshoe curve from Liskeard along which I had travelled earlier in the day. From the circular end of the jetty, which has cleverly served Thomas's purpose in stopping the little harbour from silting up, I watch a procession of rust-stained fishing boats file in one by one from the ocean, chased by squabbling seagulls. As night falls, the sea is like mercury and the horizon 'razor sharp' – to use a phrase that, in the argot of local fishermen, heralds a clear night.

On the fish quay they are beginning to unload their hoard. Here are glistening mackerel, sole, plaice, squid and conger eel, with a few of the choicest prizes, some fat, black, gleaming turbot. Weighed into boxes and covered with shovelfuls of ice to await auction early next morning, the hoard will sadly no longer travel aboard Great Western Railway fish trains up to Paddington. Instead, it will speed off in white Transit vans to Plymouth, where it will be loaded onto the Roscoff ferry, to be treasured by chefs in the smart restaurants of Brittany and Normandy. The Looe fishing fleet these days is a shadow of its former self. 'There are just seventy men working the boats here now,' the man with the shovel tells me. 'And most of us only do it to pay off the debts on our government loans. Out there' – he sweeps an arm across the horizon – 'the big Spanish trawlers are sucking the stuff up like Dysons. Another generation and we'll all be dead and gone.'

Ghosts everywhere. Somehow the Looe valley seems to be full of them – a large fluorescent cross on the tower of the ancient St Nicholas church on the quay sends out mercury-lit beams as if designed to dispel them. The town is empty as I cross the harbour to the Jolly Sailor, a nicotine-stained, low-beamed old place, where I have booked to stay the night. A notice on the bedroom wall pronounces: YOU ARE STAYING IN THE OLDEST INN IN THE TOWN OF LOOE, and I have read somewhere that it is the most haunted too. I sleep well, untroubled by the supernatural – unless you include that familiar 'peeing ghost' that can often be heard in hostelries with thin walls, usually at four in the morning. But maybe I have had a lucky escape. In the morning the landlord, Stuart Horton, tells me that his barmaid Tina has often felt a ghost tucking the sheets of her bed in behind her back while sleeping. 'We have regulars too terrified to stay in that room, and these are people in their fifties! Excuse me, I must get on, since I have a wake to organise today.' I wonder: whatever can he possibly mean?

Over at the station, the Looe Valley Line has all her finery on for the big day, which is blessed by crisp autumn sunshine. And look! Are they ghosts or are there some railway staff on the platform at Looe station – probably for the first time in decades? The two men in high-visibility jackets tell me they are here to handle the crowds. 'You'll know when the train comes down the valley,' one announces knowingly to the assembly awaiting the birthday train. 'You'll see the birds shoot up in the air. They'll be getting the fright of their lives!' And here it comes – first some wisps of steam floating above the trees, followed by a flap of birds, and then the unmistakable beat of a two-cylinder Great Western pannier tank engine. Small children cover their ears and goggle with amazement, and I overhear one curmudgeon remark, 'It's a ninety-four-hundred. Never had them down here in the old days. All they were ever fit for was shunting empty carriages at Paddington. Now what they should have provided was a forty-five-hundred Prairie tank just like in the old days.' But he is drowned out by the slamming of carriage doors as the first passengers disembark from their historic journey down from Liskeard.

There may be no modern-day equivalent of a top-hatted Isambard Kingdom Brunel or a Sir Daniel Gooch, with his gold fob watch, aboard today, but First Great Western has dispatched some of the shiniest of its top brass from Paddington in the form of directors Sue Evans and Matthew Golton, along with a crew of corporate acolytes. And, just as during that other great anniversary in 1935, they are accompanied by local mayors and a bevy of civic dignitaries. 'The train's bang on schedule. She's performed brilliantly,' Matthew tells me jubilantly. But there is another big test that everyone is waiting for. Can a steam-hauled train, the first in half a century, make it back up the valley to Looe without letting itself down – and, more importantly, 175 years of Great Western history?

To make sure all goes well there is a diesel on the back to offer a nudge if necessary, but Class 37 No. 37685, built in 1964, is not much younger than her steam sister, No. 9466, of 1947 vintage. The combined ages of the engines and their drivers, Ray Churchill on the steam footplate and Jim Tipping at the throttle of the diesel, total 237 years – sixty-two years older, on my calculation, than the GWR itself. Striking too is the fact that they all belong to a great British industrial pedigree, now regrettably almost entirely erased from our history. Designed by Frederick Hawksworth, the last chief mechanical engineer at Swindon, the pannier tank has a plate on its splasher which proclaims that it was built at the great engineering works of Robert Stephenson and Hawthorns in Newcastle upon Tyne (yes, *that* Robert Stephenson, the father of the railways), while the Class 37 was the product of another great British engineering tradition, the Vulcan Foundry works of English Electric at Newton-le-Willows in Lancashire. The drivers have no less a heritage. Ray tells me that he was one of the very last British Railways drivers to be 'passed out' for steam at Saltley depot in Birmingham is 1966, as the steam age came to an end, while Driver Jim ('Tipping as in tipping prohibited,' he tells me cheerily) was one of the last steam cleaners at Tyseley, another West Midlands shed.

Also on board, with a tear in his eye, is Cyril Willis, eighty-nine, who was the guard on the very last steam train from Liskeard to Looe on Sunday 10 September 1961, talking with a rich West Country accent that has almost competely disappeared – just like the old days of the railway that he describes. 'It was a 4500 Class engine,' he tells me. 'They usually headed the trains here because their small wheels were great for going up the incline into Liskeard. Members of the old Liskeard Drama Group came down for the last train, with people dressed in mourning black, and they put flowers on the buffers and a wreath round the engine's funnel. As I gave the signal for the train to depart, the whistle was blown at full blast and they set off detonators on the track.' His voice quavers ever so slightly.' Was it a sadness to me? In a way yes, and in a way no. Steam was what I was always used to. I started in the railway in 1937 as a lamp porter at a place called Coryton on the old line to Launceston. That's all closed now.' He rattles off a list of great West Country railway names. 'I went from there to Totnes, Totnes to Brent, Brent to Princetown. That branch was a sad loss – it closed in 1956. Then I went to Plymouth, coming here in 1953. I stayed till I retired, twenty-five years ago. When I first came here there was no road bridge over the Tamar so we used to get loaded seven-coach trains of a summer Saturday. We needed a banking engine for that. And I was busy up here. There were so many passengers that at Looe alone we had two signalmen, two porters, a checker, a lorry driver, two clerks and a station-master.'

As Cyril talks, his eyes water with a hint of regret. 'Looking back on it, I might like to have been an engine driver. But that wasn't the route to promotion in those days. I went from lamp porter, parcel porter, leading parcel porter and then guard, rising up six grades. No, don't call me a railway enthusiast. I reckon myself lucky to have got a job at all; there weren't many around in those days.'

With Ray's steady hand on the steam regulator at the front and Jim on the diesel throttle at the back, the birthday train is eased up the valley so smoothly that there is barely a rattle of the coffee cups in the buffet car, though Dennis Howells, No. 9466's owner, is sitting on his own, dressed in overalls, flat hat perched on his head, in a corner seat, looking quietly apprehensive. 'Don't confuse me with that football referee chap who they made minister for drought, which led to that terrible flooding,' he tells me. 'I bought my loco back in 1977 after she'd been in a scrapyard for years at Barry Island.' He tells me the story of the legendary Dai Woodham, a South Wales scrap merchant who almost single-handedly saved Britain's steam heritage by buying up old locomotives from British Rail-ways in the 1960s, and instead of cutting them up, sold them on to preservationists. No. 9466 is one of 213 locomotives eventually rescued from the Barry torch. 'I've rebuilt her twice from top to bottom over the years,' says Howells. 'I'm seventy-one now, and she's always given me the greatest pleasure. Yes, she's running very nicely today. See for yourself.'

I am invited to ask permission of Driver Ray to travel on the footplate as far as Liskeard – as with ships' captains the protocol surrounding an engine driver's authority is absolute – but on the way up to the front I run into another veteran of the line with a yarn to relate. Ray Pettipher, a handsome bearded man who reminds me of a seafarer, looking twenty years younger than his eighty-two years, was the last station-master at Looe, until the staff on the line were slashed in 1964. 'It was really busy when I came here,' he tells me. 'I had nine people working with me, and there were freight sidings running down onto the quay. I'd been chief clerk at Bude – I'd never been a stationmaster before. I was a bit nervous. Stationmasters were very important in those days, like the vicar or the mayor. It was a very responsible job. I had to keep an eye on everything that was going on. It was a long day, though there were fewer trains on most days than they have now. But summer was very busy. We used to get swamped with day-trippers down from Plymouth. "The play-ground of Plymouth", that's what they used to call Looe.

'One day *Candid Camera* [a popular TV series in which pranks were played on people and filmed with a secret camera] came here with this pantomime cow they wanted to go on the train. My clerk Cyril didn't know what to do. But I kept a straight face and told them they would have to pay two fares – for both the front and hind legs of the cow. That spoiled their fun! We had a lovely old station, with a wooden canopy to shelter the passengers till they knocked it down in 1968. The word "Looe" was picked out in flower beds – lovingly maintained, they were. We had roaring fires in both the waiting room and the porters' room in those days. People used to hang around the station just to enjoy the warmth.'

Up on the footplate, Ray, a lean man with a red necker-chief tied rakishly over his blue overalls, handles his engine with the gravitas of one who knows he is among the very last standard bearers of a skill that goes back even beyond the foundation of the Great Western, to the day in 1804 when a famous Cornishman called Richard Trevithick drove the world's first ever working steam locomotive. With a gentle tap on the regulator here and a touch on the brakes there, the train rumbles into Coombe Junction Halt, where

Ray needs the help of his fireman to move the heavy red reverser lever for the train to climb up to Liskeard. Now it is Jim's diesel that will take the strain. 'Go easy, Jim,' Ray says over the walkie-talkie. 'We could get a bit of slipping on the way up.' But now the heat is off – literally – the firebox doors can be closed, the shovel rested. At the buffers in Liskeard Ray mops his brow and leans out of his cab ruminatively in the way engine drivers have done since the dawn of steam. I don't like to ask him whether he is contemplating the mighty sweep of the 175-year heritage of the Great Western Railway or simply the prospect of a refreshing cup of tea.

All of a sudden the passengers have departed and the platform is deserted. The dignitaries and townsfolk of Liskeard are heading home for their supper, and the Looe Valley Line is returning to its slumbers. With a rattle of exhaust and a clank from the coupling rods, the empty train backs out on its way to the sidings for the night. Here is that perfect image of the Great Western we all like to recall – wisps of steam in a clear blue sky, the chocolate and cream coaches, a shiny green pannier tank on a idyllic branch line, the last rays of the setting sun glinting off its copper-capped chimney. God's Wonderful Railway, certainly. But also – for everyone who has enjoyed its 175th birthday today – Gone With Regret.

Will another steam train return here in the next fifty years? Who knows? As night starts to fall, the Liskeard signalman slides open the panelled window of his old wooden signal box and gives me a wave, remembering our conversation of the previous day. And as the ancient wooden signal rattles down on Liskeard's main line platform for my train, which will head home through the grimy inner London suburbs to Paddington, I think of Bernard Moore's poem 'A Cornish Chorus', one of the most evocative, I reckon, ever written about a country branch line.

Peckham Rye, Loughborough, Elephant, St Paul's
Every morning the porter bawls.
The train grinds out and I gaze on lots
Of sad back gardens and chimney pots
Factory stacks and smoky haze
Showering smuts on the close-packed ways

But trapped and prisoned as I may be,
I lift a latch and my thoughts go free,
And once again I am running down
On a winding track from a Cornish town
And I dream the names of the stations through –
'Moorswater, Causeland, Sandplace, Looe' . . .

The line twists down through patches sweet
Of soft green pasture and waving wheat
And the stream spreads out to a river wide
Where ships creep up at the turn of tide,
Till a tangle of stars on a blue sky spun
Gives me the sign of a journey done,
And I stand contented on the quay
And hear the surging song of the sea.

So runs the dreamlike journey through,
'Moorswater, Causeland, Sandplace, Looe';
But every morning the porter bawls,
'Peckham Rye, Loughborough, Elephant, St Paul's.'

'We're neither of us free to love each other': Famous words, spoken by Celia Johnson to Trevor Howard on the platform at Carnforth in David Lean's 1945 film *Brief Encounter*, helped transform a Lancashire junction into one of the world's most romantic settings.

CHAPTER FOUR

THE 10.34 FROM MORECAMBE – A BRIEF ENCOUNTER WITH THE 'SECRET' TRAIN OVER THE PENNINES

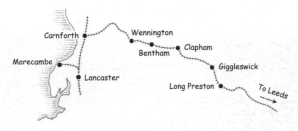

Morecambe to Leeds via Carnforth, Bentham, Giggleswick and Long Preston

Some train journeys should only be viewed in grainy black and white, and this is one of them. It's 1944 and we're on a darkened station platform in Lancashire. The emotion is running high and the atmosphere is steamy in every sense. Here are Alec and Laura (aka Trevor Howard and Celia Johnson) locked in tearful embrace as they await the train at 'Milford Junction'. The platform clock, now an icon for cinema buffs across the world, is ticking away on their doomed relationship. The Noël Coward dialogue is in the clipped accents of *Movietone News*: 'I want you to promise me something. That no matter how unhappy you are, you'll meet me again next Thursday . . .' Cue the welling tones of Rachmaninov's Second Piano Concerto.

More than half a century on, I'm wiping away a tear along with some of the other patrons of the Carnforth station visitors' centre, as the video of David Lean's famous film goes round on an endless loop in the little cinema on Platform 1. These days a modern Trevor and Celia would not be able to get a main-line train, no matter how long they waited, from the station that doubled as the setting for one of the weepiest goodbyes in movie history. The clock, still bearing the legend 'Joyce of Whitchurch', has been restored and hangs just above the stairs to the underpass as it did in the film. The tea urns in the refreshment room, scene of the couple's illicit encounters, are still sizzling. But the London-to-Scotland trains whoosh through at 100 mph, and the platform where Trevor and Celia embraced is fenced off.

But don't fret. For those in the know it's still possible to take one of Britain's most spectacular rail journeys from the little stone-built station in this handsome north Lancashire town. It's a line with just five trains a day, and who would bet that more than a handful of people outside the remote Pennine villages through which it passes on its two-hour-and-thirteen-minute journey to West Yorkshire would ever know it still exists. But thank goodness. There are fewer lovelier and more authentic journeys through the best of rural Britain than this one.

For around a century the Morecambe–Leeds route was a railway busy with expresses and stopping trains. In its glory days the farming communities in the spectacular countryside along the line were within easy reach of the great cities of Lancashire and Yorkshire, and mill workers from the West Riding poured in their hundreds of thousands to resorts on the Lancashire coast. Late trains on Saturday night brought revellers home from dances in Morecambe's Central Pier ballroom, and in summer labourers from Ireland crossed the sea to Heysham and travelled for 'hiring day' in the great sheep and cattle market at Bentham. Hikers headed for Bell Busk station, the gateway to Malhamdale, and the more energetic to Clapham, where they could hoof it up Ingleborough. Each tiny station had its own goods yard and cattle dock – all gone now, as have nearly all the little wooden signal boxes – but the line is still with us, and its charms are the most underrated in Britain.

I started my seventy-mile journey early this morning by the seaside in Morecambe. The statue of Eric Morecambe (né Bartholomew), the town's most famous son, is frozen in permanent jollity on the promenade, but there doesn't seem a lot to celebrate in the Lancashire resort this windy May day. The tide appears to have gone out in every sense. Both piers have been destroyed – one by fire and the other by the waves – and all that is visible of the closed Frontierland pleasure park, which once dominated the seafront, is the derelict Polo tower. (Perhaps ironic that this was once an advertising totem for the 'mint with the hole'; now it dominates a hole in the middle of Morecambe.) There's nobody much around: just the gulls and a chilly breeze, and me.

It was the railways that were the making and breaking of Lancashire's second-favourite resort, though many proud north Lancastrians still believe they are first in a league that includes Blackpool and Southport. The trains transformed a little fishing village called Poulton-le-Sands into a seaside destination on an industrial scale, bringing weary West Riding mill workers in their hundreds of thousands for their Wakes Week holidays, to enjoy some candyfloss and a bit of kiss-me-quick on the breezy fringes of Morecambe Bay. The town's boarding houses ('hot and cold running water and interior sprung mattresses in all rooms') resounded with the dialects of Heckmondwike, Halifax, Huddersfield and Hebden Bridge. Never mind that the landladies were as grim as Thora Hird, the comic actress who was one of Morecambe's most famous daughters. You could rely on Lancashire's finest funny men George Formby, Jimmy Clitheroe and Eric Morecambe to keep you entertained.

No wonder the Midland Railway plonked its commodious stone-built station smack in the middle of the seafront and called it Morecambe Promenade. It is still proudly there, although these days there are no trains, since it closed in 1994, and the station has been partly converted into a Kentucky Fried Chicken and a pub ('two steaks and a Viennetta for

£10'). Where holidaymakers once queued for tickets home to Huddersfield and Harrogate, there is an 'arts centre' with posters advertising 'We'll meet again – Britain's best wartime nostalgia show'. Meanwhile, rail travellers must walk a quarter of a mile through a shopping mall to where the line has been truncated to a single island platform.

The solitary building in the new station, although clean and modern, is smaller than the gents' toilets in the former Promenade station. (Old-style compartment coaches without corridors, combined with plentiful crates of ale, led to huge pent-up demand for simultaneous relief on arrival at seaside termini.) Next door, in the vast area where summer Saturday excursion trains disgorged their passengers to feast on Morecambe's entertainments, are those identikit icons of the modern leisure industry – Homebase, Morrisons and Aldi. Here it is possible, in recession-hit Morecambe, to buy a bottle of British 'white wine' for £1.99 and a chip roll for 50p. Even the statues of seabirds, built along the seafront to cheer the place up, look a bit dejected.

But there's plenty of reason to smile. Eric Morecambe is perpetually in 'Bring Me Sunshine' mode and the magnificent views across Morecambe Bay to the Lakeland fells are as sensational as ever. And here in this unlikely setting is as superb a building to start a railway journey as any in the land after London's St Pancras station. Although the departure of railway business may have sucked the life out of Morecambe, a monument to the heyday of the railway is bringing it back again, in the form of the revived Midland Hotel. For years this great white Art Deco building perched on the edge of the shingle, opened by the London Midland and Scottish Railway in 1933, rotted away into semi-dereliction. It was a blight on the seafront, and in desperation locals secretly hoped that one night a tsunami might creep up and sweep it into the ocean.

In 2003 it was bought by Manchester property developers Urban Splash, who have restored it as close as possible to architect Oliver Hill's original design, when it was the last word in modernistic luxury. The *Architectural Review* described it as 'in complete harmony with its natural surroundings . . . it rises from the sea like a great white ship, gracefully curved.' Most splendid of all is the huge bas-relief in the hotel's entrance lounge, carved by sculptor Eric Gill from six tonnes of Portland stone. The original design, showing a naked Odysseus stepping from the sea to be greeted by the goddess Nausicaa, surrounded by naked youths and maidens, was too sexually explicit for the prudish directors of the London, Midland and Scottish Railway and had to be toned down.

Still, there's even more luxurious escapism to be savoured as I fortify myself with a hearty Lancashire breakfast in the sun lounge for the journey ahead. Screw up your eyes just for a moment as you stare up at the spiral stairs, described by *Country Life* as 'a fairy staircase one would willingly climb until it reached to heaven', and imagine yourself at the next table to Wallis Simpson, Noël Coward, Winston Churchill, Gloria Vanderbilt or any of the other celebrity clients of the LMS who came to soak up the sun in the Midland's 1930s heyday.

Not so many pleasures on offer walking through the shopping mall to today's diminished Morecambe station. Nor aboard the 10.34 to Leeds, a modest 'Class 156' two-coach diesel train which hasn't been cleaned very effectively from the night before. On my seat is a flier advertising 'Free dance in the Blue Coyote strip sports saloon, Leeds'. But never mind. Northern Rail, the franchise operator, and a band of local volunteers work against the odds to keep this lovely and most secret line across the Pennines going. The 10.34 is the first through train of the day, and no one seems in much of a rush. Gone are the days of the Leeds, Bradford and Morecambe Residential, when the resort was the home of West Riding wool magnates who could leave on the 07.42 'Resi', flick through the stock prices in early editions of the *Yorkshire Post* in padded armchairs in special club cars and be in their offices at Bradford Forster

Square by 09.15. But who cares? We are on time, picking up speed past the rows of little 'Dunroamin' retirement bunga-lows that are a hallmark of modern Morecambe and onto the first stop at Bare Lane, where the signalman in his 1930s wooden box hands over the token to permit the driver to go ahead on the single track.

But hold on a minute. Instead of heading for the high Pennines and the West Riding on the direct line far ahead, our train is turning south along the West Coast Main Line to Lancaster. Did the driver pick up the wrong token? Have the points been mis-set? Not exactly. What happened to the lines around More-cambe in the mid-1960s was either Beeching's worst bungle or a masterstroke, a deliberately engineered and Machiavellian plan to drive away passengers from this beautiful railway. Not so far-fetched – this was a standard tactic of the Beeching-era 1960s.

The Little North Western Line, called Little to distinguish it from the bigger and grander London and North Western Railway trunk route from Euston, was promoted in the railway mania of 1845. The idea was to build a main-line route from the Midlands and West Riding to Carlisle and Scotland. There were to be two main branches: one would run from Leeds to Ingleton in the Yorkshire Dales, connecting to the Euston–Glasgow main line at Low Gill; the other was to be a direct line over the Pennines to Lancaster and Morecambe. Despite an economic crisis caused by failed corn and potato harvests, both eventually got built, even though the stress wrecked the health of chief engineer Thomas Gooch, elder brother of Sir Daniel Gooch, the distinguished locomotive engineer of the Great Western Railway.

The two branches survived until the 1960s. Though the Little North Western's newer big brother, the Settle and Carlisle, had taken away much of the northbound traffic, the Ingleton route was used for diversions during heavy snowfalls and other blockages. But Beeching was having no truck with these slow scenic routes to the far north, and the axe was scheduled to fall on both. But in a final gesture of Grand Guignol, the British Railways chairman also passed a death sentence on the direct line to Lancaster, at the same time killing off the suburban electric trains between Lancaster, Morecambe and the port of Heysham. It mattered not a hoot to the chairman that this service of fast and frequent trains, inaugurated in 1908, was a pioneer for the overhead electrified lines that are now standard across the world, and once operated a speedier service than the London Underground.

But even Beeching realised he couldn't get away with shutting the entire line at a stroke, so he cut out the direct route through Lancaster, forcing the Morecambe trains to zigzag north to a junction at Carnforth, simultaneously firing the booking office staff at Carnforth station. It was the classic technique of 'Drive 'em away and shut 'em down.' Passengers attempting to get to the county's main centres of Lancaster and Preston were forced to endure the sort of timetable test set by William Temple, Archbishop of Canterbury, when he was headmaster of Repton School. The great man used to sentence badly behaved boys to a special form of imposition. He would produce a copy of *Bradshaw's Railway Guide* and order the offender to find the quickest way of travelling from, say, Penrith to Ipswich. The hapless boy had to write down all the times of arrival and departure at every point of change. Temple, who had memorised the timetable in its entirety, would arrive at the designated destination on average about an hour ahead, with a resultant clip round the ear, or worse, for the unfortunate youth.

However, even the great Archbishop Temple would probably have been defeated by the complexities of the Beeching plan. Local protesters eventually got the trains to stop at Lancaster again, though not without forcing passengers from Morecambe to travel south and then north along the same tracks, back to where they came from. Which is why we are, somewhat absurdly, at the buffers in the bay platform in Lancaster, and the guard and driver are swapping places to speed back in reverse down the line to Carnforth.

Still, there are compensations. Lancaster station is always full of interest, partly because it lives splendidly up to its former name of Lancaster Castle, with turrets reflecting the castle on the hill up above, home of the Pendle witchcraft trials. There is even ivy growing with Gothic authenticity over the platform buildings. But maybe it is the presence of students from Lancaster University, who always dominate the platforms in large numbers – delightful though Lancaster is, the bright lights are always somewhere else. Cheery too, as we rattle north, whipped by the 125 mph vortex of passing Pendolino trains, are the shocking-pinks of the cherry trees and stark yellows of the hillside gorse, blazing brilliantly after one of the coldest winters for more than fifty years. Observant passengers can tell we are approaching Carnforth by the vast Valhalla of super-annuated rusting railway carriages in the sidings to the left of the line. This is the headquarters of the West Coast Railway Company, whose boss David Smith has almost single-handedly ensured the continued running of preserved steam on the main lines in Britain, holding a rare 'safety case' – a legal require-ment for any company wanting to drive century-old steam locos on the same tracks as inter-city expresses.

Like many collectors of paraphernalia, it seems that Smith cannot quite relinquish some of his ancient charges to the scrapyard, and they are left to slumber, weeds entangling the bogies and couplings. Smith is also custodian of the last coaling tower in Britain, which dominates the town and is a reminder of the fact that Carnforth shed housed some of the final steam locomotives on the network when regular main-line steam came to an end in 1968. Towers such as this once rose like great concrete campaniles over industrial towns and cities across Britain. Many Carnforth visitors opt for an older attrac-tion by taking an excursion to the local White Scar Cave, which includes in its limestone tunnels the 200,000-year-old Battlefield Cavern. Over 330 feet long, its roof soaring to 100 feet high and covered with thousands of delicate stalactites, this is one of the true geological wonders of Europe.

Until recently it might have been difficult to get any directions to the cave from the unstaffed station at Carnforth. Dank and semi-derelict, it lived only in memory as one of the greatest and busiest junctions in Lancashire. But a group of enthusiasts raised £1.5 million to transform it into a 'heritage centre', recreating the wartime atmosphere of David Lean's famous film, including the famous refreshment room where Trevor Howard first stared into Celia Johnson's eyes. Now, as well as being able to book a train ticket again, you can buy a *Brief Encounter* postcard, video, tea towel, key ring and a set of *Brief Encounter* place mats, as well as having a *Brief Encounter* lunch in the *Brief Encounter* refreshment room 'It's our fourth time here,' explain Keith and Maureen from Shipley, who are sitting next to me in the cinema, 'and we love the atmosphere.' Maureen's mum was Celia Johnson's greatest fan – 'her eyes were just so beautiful' – and Keith is a bit of a movie buff himself. 'It's a little-known fact,' he tells me, 'that they were originally going to film it at Watford Junction, but it was too busy, so the Ministry of War told David Lean he'd have to settle for Carnforth. Did you know that when the drivers of the expresses saw the arc lights on the platform during the war blackout, they slowed down? This was no good at all, so Lean sent the word down the line to speed up again. Some of the drivers saw this a licence to let rip. You should have seen those engines go!'

There seems no limit to Keith's knowledge: 'And would you believe the clock had a false face so that the hands could be set to film time? Or that Stanley Holloway, the ticket collector, was so nervous about his part in having to cross the line that a double had to stand in for him?' It turns out too that the *Brief Encounter* tearoom was not real either. Lean didn't like the location, which was too far from the running lines, so the exterior was constructed from flats further down the platform. The interior scenes were shot at Denham studios, so today's Carnforth version had to be reconstructed from photographs and may be the only railway cafe in the world designed from a black-and-white video. Still it looks authentic enough, though one wonders whether Laura might have enjoyed the *Brief Encounter* coffee or what Alec would have made of the sweet potato and red pepper soup. I settle for a cup of 'railway tea'. Rose, who is serving today, isn't sure what this is but directs me to a book on the counter called *The Lancashire Teapot Trail*. I simply say, 'Strong.'

But it's time for the next train, which is already pulling into the platform. There's quite a crowd waiting for the 13.58 to Leeds, mostly schoolchildren sitting on their oversize rucksacks monogrammed with *Thomas* and *Barbie* logos. 'We're on our way to school camp,' a small girl explains excitedly. But to me there's something potentially even more special in prospect – the arrival of the Boat Train, the one service each way a day that connects with the Isle of Man ferry at Heysham. Although when it comes jolting into the platform it is one of the most improbable boat trains to be seen anywhere in Britain, consisting of a two-coach Pacer train made from old 1980s bus parts to which has been tagged a single Class 153 railcar dating from the same decade. What a far cry from the line's heyday when this would have been the Belfast Boat Express or its successor the Ulster Express, speeding up the line to St Pancras or Euston. The Ulster Express was especially grand. With its crimson and silver headboard and often a crack Royal Scot locomotive on the front, this was one of the star named trains of Britain, offering a through service from London to Belfast of just over twelve hours. To ease the journey, pre-war passengers were provided with a special lounge car, complete with leather armchairs.

'Boat trains and mail trains have something others haven't

got, even though externally they may be indistinguishable from the rest,' wrote Roger Lloyd in his essay *Travelling Hopefully*, referring to the glamour of these often exotic services. The 13.58 certainly has something, though probably not what Lloyd had in mind. Nevertheless, travelling hopefully is certainly the watchword for the Leeds service this lunchtime, as the train takes the curve to cross the West Coast Main Line towards Leeds with wheels shrieking. The Ulster Expresses ended in 1975 when the ferries were withdrawn because of the Irish Troubles, and the notorious Pacer units were introduced at a time of British Rail austerity in the 1980s. It is a curious fact about the British railway system in 2011 that there are still trains with just four wheels per carriage in the style of the coaches drawn by the *Rocket* at the dawn of the railway age in 1830. The wheel arrangement of the Pacers was already obsolete in the 1870s, yet here we are plodding along in primitive fashion in the era of the Eurostar and TGV. In fact, I can state with authority that the *Rocket*'s coaches were rather more comfortable, since a month previously I had ridden behind a full-scale replica of the train run by the Science Museum on a specially constructed track by the Albert Memorial in London.

Still, the school party is having a jolly time treating the corridor connection like a trampoline as the train bucks and kicks over the track. My carriage is so full that I'm standing – well, trying to stand. As he squeezes past while the Pacer traverses a particularly rough piece of track, Alan the ticket collector overbalances with his heavy ticket machine. He says, 'Trouble is these trains were designed for welded rails and this line is old-fashioned "diddly-dee, diddly-da" track all the way. But there's one thing about a Pacer – you get a great view through the windows. Have you been on the Settle and Carlisle, by the way? Well, I reckon this line is just as good. We're just waiting to be discovered.'

And the scenery, across the empty rolling hills, is spectacular. This is sheep country and today lambs are everywhere – black lambs, white lambs, fat woolly lambs and scrawny shorn ones. We cross the Lancaster Canal and the sparkling waters of the River Keer, passing through the little closed stations at Borwick, Arkholm and Melling, shut even before Beeching. Ironically, more of the charming original gabled architecture of the line survives here than at the stations still in service, since with these almost every element of architectural interest was razed to the ground in the austerities that came later. There are no signal boxes or signals either, since the twenty-four-mile stretch of line here is the longest block section (span of distance between signals) in Britain. After the 1,230-yard Melling Tunnel, the train emerges at the little station of Wennington, where at last we join the old main line after the diversion from Morecambe. No one gets on or off here, so Alan presses the buzzer and we are speedily on our way. Now the train is climbing towards its summit, crossing and re-crossing the River Wenning on a succession of impressive bridges and viaducts and passing across the invisible border between Lancashire and Yorkshire.

The next stop, Bentham, is as authentic a country town as you could find anywhere in Britain: nothing too obviously pretty but a workaday place making a good living out of farming and its own industries. All very North Yorkshire, and no pretensions here, thank you very much. The town is home to one of the biggest sheep and cattle auctions in the north of England, and so fast is the bidding that unwary outsiders are warned not to scratch their noses, otherwise there is a risk of being accompanied by some unwanted pets on the way home. The station area is dominated by a large factory housing one of the world's top manufacturers of fire hosepipes – not such an oddity as this might appear, since the process of weaving flax into tubes was invented by a mill owner in Bentham in the nineteenth century

But there's a pretty and well-tended garden on the platform packed with lupins, love-lies-bleeding and troughs of pansies.

There's also a cheerful little mural with a text that reads, '150 years of the Morecambe–Leeds line, via Lunesdale, Wenning-dale, Ribbledale and Airedale 1850–2000'. No wonder so much care is lavished here, since Bentham is home to some of the fiercest guardians of the Leeds–Morecambe line. Chief among them is David Alder, the postmaster, who keeps an eagle eye on the railway from his eyrie at Bentham post office. It's a steep climb to the top of the hill, past the butcher and the little baker – so traditional-looking that you can half-see the Hovis delivery boy walking alongside over the cobbles, pushing his bike loaded with loaves. Are those the strains of the Brig-house and Rastrick Brass Band playing the *New World Symphony* on the breeze? In the sitting room of the post office, piled high with railway books, maps and timetables, Alder is wistful for the old days. 'All the freight trains over the line went completely after they shut the chemicals plant at Heysham. The bitumen trains that used to be a staple of the line have gone too. Then, ten years ago, they dealt us the Blow. They cut the passenger service from seven trains a day to four. They said it was because they didn't have enough diesel units to go round. We users of the line got together and they gave us one back. So now we have five.' Alder goes through his files and presents me with a beautifully printed guide to the village. 'But today they say that if we want more trains, they'll have to turn them round at Skipton and they'd no longer go on to Leeds. We're utterly, utterly opposed They're trying to turn us from a main line into a branch line . . .'

But the queue for pensions and postal orders is getting ever longer as we talk, and I have to go too, because I mustn't miss the last train of the day. Alder waves me goodbye, and on the way down to the station in the Wenning valley I read his little book, which contains an undated anonymous poem, probably never studied in university departments of English literature but with a profound resonance in this beautiful landscape.

Down by the Wenning and the railway station there's just

time before the train arrives to inspect the little parish church of St Margaret, where there's a memorial in the sanctuary to one Hornby Roughsedge, a founder of the Little North Western. No wonder the retired vicar, John Bearpark, is the main cheer-leader for the line's users' group, since the tracks pass so close to the church that in the railway's busiest days the roar of steam and the clatter of the carriages must have drowned out the sermons of the most hellfire-inclined of vicars. 'It was the weddings that were the worst,' Bearpark tells me, 'since there were more trains on a Saturday.' But the muffling of many an 'I do' did not deter the Reverend John. 'We lived on one side of the track and the church was on the other. So I was able to observe the trains at all times. In fact, it's been a lifelong attach-ment. My aunt owned a boarding house in Morecambe, and my wife and I have just celebrated our fiftieth wedding anniver-sary with a night in the Midland Hotel.'

The chill of an early Pennine evening is closing in as the 16.58 to Leeds arrives. The next stage of the journey becomes steadily bleaker as we climb into the Pennines. Here sheep and drystone walls increasingly dominate the landscape as the vege-tation gets sparser. At the start of my journey, in the softer Morecambe climate, the trees were merrily breaking bud. Here, as we climb into the bleak moorland, the buds of the daffodils are still clenched closed. My only companions in the carriage are a party of middle-aged men in very jolly mood. They tell me they are farmers from Bentham and are off to watch Leeds play at Elland Road. Big men, ruddy-faced York-shire country types, I ask them – since there will be no trains back – how they are going to get home. 'We'll get back somehow – probably hitch a lift.' Yes, they'd like a better train service. 'But we're Yorkshiremen. Nowt bothers us.'

Clapham, the next station, is a lonely place indeed. Once this was known as Clapham Junction. Not to be confused with Clapham Junction in south London, which as every schoolboy knows is the busiest station in Britain, Clapham in North Yorkshire must be among the least busy. Today's passengers, though sadly there are none joining or alighting this afternoon, have only a couple of 1960s bus shelters to protect them from the winds whipping off the hillsides. Even so, Clapham must count itself lucky still to have its former stationmaster's house on the up platform. With its mock-Tudor architecture, it is now a cosy private residence. But what a view. Here, imposing its vast presence on the landscape, is the brooding summit of Ingleborough, the most famous of the Yorkshire Dales' Three Peaks. Discerning walkers know that Clapham station is the place to start the classic five-hour hike through Trow Gill and Gaping Gill, but stay on the train for the next leg of the journey and the mountain views of Ingleborough, Whernside and Penyghent in profile through the left window of our Pacer are among the most spectacular in Britain.

The landscape begins to soften again as the train reaches Giggleswick, once lampooned in the BBC sitcom *Hancock's Half Hour* as the sort of obscure place where travelling actors might fetch up, though it was more famously associated with chat show host Russell Harty, who was in a previous life an English teacher at Giggleswick school. Soon there is a clattering of points as the train runs onto the Settle–Carlisle Line, past the magnificently restored Midland Railway signal box at Settle Junction – all gleaming weatherboarding and maroon and cream paint.

The sun is setting as I alight at Long Preston, the first station beyond the junction. Now we are within the commuter hinterland of Leeds, though this stern stone-built village is no suburbia. The community is famous for its grand village greens and its annual maypole festival, though less so for the amenities of its station, where everything, including the footbridge and the timetable notice, appears to have been demolished. Tonight the chomping sheep nudging at the fence outnumber the passengers. Still, I have a treat in store – staying the night in the B & B over the post office, where Julie and Arthur Modd are fans of the railway and preside over the posts, postal orders and newsagency, though it is a long time since bundles of newspapers arrived with a *thud* on the platform via the morning train from Leeds. Over delicious kippers next morning, Julie tells me, 'We get quite a few walkers come here off the railway. But isn't it a terrible shame they let the buildings go?'

I can't help but agree, since there's a chilly wind curling along the platform at Long Preston that morning. How cosy it would be to snuggle in front of a blazing waiting-room fire. But now I must ponder my options. Should I go on to Hellifield and Skipton, taking the final leg into Leeds, which is no longer the exclusive territory of the Little North Western, as it shares the tracks from here on with trains from the Settle and Carlisle line and further on with the suburban electric services that run through Airedale? Would one more ticket sold for the through train to Leeds tip the balance towards saving the service for the future? But I decide to head back west where I have come from, taking the line back up into the hills, where the rails are already shining blood-red with the rising sun. Here, I'm told, it is possible still to take the route of the old direct line from Wennington to Morecambe, closed during the slaughter of the 1960s. Not by train, but on foot, since the trackbed between Caton and Lancaster has been transformed into a footpath and cycleway. After a taxi ride from Wennington and a pint of real ale in the Station Hotel at Caton, one of that sad legion of station hotels across the land that no longer have a station to keep them company, I stride along the final six miles into Lancaster through a landscape once painted by Turner and declared 'perfect' by the poet Thomas Gray.

Could this beautiful valley, of which Ruskin said, 'I do not know in all my country a place more naturally divine,' ever be observed once again from a railway carriage window? Sadly not, however much Postmaster Alder and the Reverend Bearpark might wish it. The route into Lancaster can never be revived, since the city's Greyhound Bridge, which once carried the trains across the Lune into the city, has been converted into a road. To this day conspiracy theorists believe this was the real reason the line was closed in the first place. Nearly half a century on, we shall almost certainly never find out, but one thing is certain: what remains of the Little North Western provides one of the most glorious train journeys in Britain for those who take the trouble to discover it.

Pastoral in commuterland: A solitary passenger waits on a sultry afternoon at Ridgmont in Bedfordshire in June 2010. The Marston Vale Line offers a timeless journey through sleepy villages and rural landscapes not far from the fringes of semi-detached London.

CHAPTER FIVE

THE 10.58 FROM BEDFORD – A PILGRIM'S PROGRESS VIA THE 'BRAIN TRAIN' TO BLETCHLEY

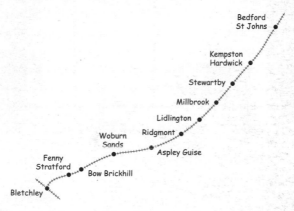

Bedford St Johns to Bletchley, via Kempston Hardwick, Stewartby, Millbrook, Ridgmont, Woburn Sands, Bow Brickhill and Fenny Stratford

Isn't it odd, the connection between religion and the railways? The most famous railway book of all, *The Adventures of Thomas the Tank Engine*, was written by a clergyman, the Reverend Wilbert Awdry. And some of the finest photographs of trains ever taken came from the lens of the Right Reverend Eric Treacy, Bishop of Wakefield, known as the Railway Bishop, who passed from this earth on Appleby station while photographing the *Evening Star*, the last steam locomotive to be built by British Railways. The unfortunate bishop suffered a heart attack, but it is as certain as can be that he is now watching over his favourite Settle–Carlisle line from a suitable vantage point in a railway heaven.

When Brunel designed Paddington station, he said he wanted

it to be like a cathedral. Cardinal Newman, beatified by the Pope in the autumn of 2010, was said to have been a rail enthusiast and may even be the first proper saint of the railway age, though many railway locomotives over the years have been named after saints. Not long ago I acquired the nameplate from one of them – *St Edmund* – removed from a very humble Freightliner Class 86 electric locomotive when it went for scrap. I bought it to mark the birth of my son, who bears the same forename. So far, no miracles can be reported, although some proclaim that the connection between God and trains is ordained in the Scriptures themselves, citing Isaiah 6, verses 1–6: 'I saw the Lord sitting upon a throne . . . and his train filled the Temple . . . and the Temple filled with smoke.'

This morning I've got John Bunyan's *The Pilgrim's Progress* on my mind. Written in 1658, it was for centuries the best-read book in Britain after the Bible. I'm lost on the fringes of Bedford, looking for a little railway station called Bedford St Johns. I know it's named after St John's church, whose rectory features in Bunyan's book as the House of the Interpreter: '"Sir," said Christian, "I was told that if I called here you would show me excellent things, such as to be a help to me on my journey . . ."' Help for the journey? There's none for me this morning since Bedford must be the worst-signposted town in Britain. I try in the huge Wetherspoon's pub called *The Pilgrim's Progress* with its ceiling frieze exhorting early-morning boozers to take the journey 'from vice to virtue'. No joy here in any sense of the word. I ask for directions in the Bunyan Museum, where an attendant shows me a Bunyan waxwork, a reconstruction of Bunyan's house, the cell door of Bunyan's prison and editions of Bunyan's famous book in 170 languages. But Bedford St Johns station? 'Hmm. I'm not really sure . . .'

Eventually I stumble across it, on the other side of the bypass and through a factory car park – just a single platform with shelter, whose acrylic windows have become opaque from being constantly cleaned of graffiti. Yet this uninspiring place is the gateway to one of the most charming and obscure country rail-ways in the land. Climb aboard the little single-coach train and you are in a parallel universe to the semi-detached Britain that marches almost all the way to London. The Marston Vale Line pursues a timeless journey through sleepy Bedfordshire and Buckinghamshire landscapes. At either extremity, the Pendolinos and HSTs (High Speed Trains) whoosh north on the West Coast and Midland main lines, and the route is bisected by the busy M1. But in between, on a journey of just over sixteen miles, stopping at all stations, we can dawdle and downshift from the modern world. So little known is this gem buried away in commuterland that the snooty booking clerk at St Pancras claimed no knowledge of it when I set off from London. The conversation is straight out of *Alice's Adventures in Wonderland*.

Me: Single to Fenny Stratford, please.
SBC: Never heard of it. You mean Stratford? You're better off taking the Tube.
Me: No, it's on the line via Bedford.
SBC: Well, Stratford-upon-Avon then?
Me: No, Fenny Stratford
SBC: Are you trying to be funny?

No wonder that the line has suffered more closure attempts than almost any other in the Home Counties. It is now a shadow of the lengthy cross-country artery it once was, running between the two great university cities of Oxford and Cambridge, although ironically it was never proposed for closure by Beeching, who saw its potential as part of a long-distance freight network. (He wasn't wrong about everything.) For generations the 'Varsity Line' with its Brain Trains, as they were nicknamed, shuttled Britain's finest intellects, with their corduroy jackets and battered briefcases, back and forth in comfort with no need to go through London and divert their minds from higher things. But razor-suited British Rail accountants up at HQ were unsentimental about the needs of a few crusty academics, and the Brain Trains came to a sad end on the last day of 1967. Seventy-seven miles of track closed, and only the section in the middle, from Bedford to Bletchley, survived. Even this has had some narrow squeaks since. It was only saved from another closure attempt in 1972 because the replacement bus operators couldn't get their act together.

Today's service, the 10.58 from Bedford to Bletchley, is not an elegant B16 4-6-0 locomotive marching up the line in plumes of steam at the head of six corridor coaches, as might have been the case in the 1940s before closure of the Oxford and Cambridge sections. Instead it is a little Class 153 single-unit railcar, modest but smart in the stylish green and black livery of London Midland, a name poached from the London, Midland and Scottish Railway, which operated the line until nationalisation in 1948. Slick private outfits they may be, but modern train firms are not averse to weaving in a bit of heritage if they think it makes them sound less corporate.

Looking back round the curve from the station as we head towards Bletchley I can see the weed-covered tracks of the line from Cambridge, destined never to reopen because of bypasses and housing estates built where the rails once were. But don't look back; there are rare pleasures ahead. 'No line could be more typically cross country,' wrote Roger Lloyd in his 1952 book *The Fascination of Railways*,

> than the Bletchley to Cambridge branch of the LMS. Travellers on that line know all about the art of making haste slowly – they have to. Its trains meander in a dreamy way through a succession of village stations whose names are poems, and in spring they run through field after field where the buttercups drench the grass making it green-gold. Like most cross-country trains they have but two speeds, slow and stop. When the buttercups are out (and I know no part of England where they flower more bravely)

the sloth of a train should matter to no one, for all can look at the fields and be satisfied.

Satisfying it certainly is. As the train passes under the Bedford southern bypass we are soon able to sample some of this countryside, and very quickly arrive at Kempston Hardwick, the first of a roll-call of stations that sound as though they are out of John Betjeman or Flanders and Swann – Stewartby, Millbrook, Lidlington, Ridgmont. Aspley Guise, Woburn Sands, Bow Brickhill and Fenny Stratford. Until recently Kempston Hardwick was one of the least used stations on the rail network, and TV crews would turn up regularly to feature it in 'just fancy that' fillers for slow news days. But it is a plucky survivor, like the rest of this remaining section of line. Opened in 1846 by the London and Birmingham Railway, it was the first railway into Bedford. But the line was left without a proper role when the Midland Railway built its own direct route into London and has become decreasingly important ever since. Even as long ago as 1905, curious little 'railmotor' trains were drafted in to bring down costs, including a Heath Robinson contraption called a Micheline, which was a lorry cab attached to a railway coach, the whole thing bouncing along the line on pneumatic tyres – thus its name.

Shortly after leaving Kempston Hardwick, on the left side of the track, is a clear area of land, once the site of the Coronation Brickworks. The Marston Vale has a long history of manufacturing bricks, and at one time the London Brick Company's factories along here were the largest in the world. If you live in a brick-built house in London, the chances are that the bricks came from hereabouts. The factories used Lower Oxford Clay – which contains seaweed as well as the fossils of all sorts of prehistoric creatures, including traces of dinosaur eggs – formed 150 million years ago, when it was part of the seabed. Thrifty for the factory owners, since the combustible elements in the clay speeded up the firing.

But the local brick industry, whose furnaces and working

conditions gave John Bunyan's puritanical successors so much scope to preach about the evils of the Industrial Revolution, is no more – extinct as the dinosaurs because it was unable to comply with modern rules on sulphur dioxide emissions. As we pass Stewartby brickworks, closed in 2008, track engineers are busy lifting the sidings, which were once busy dispatching Bedford bricks all across the land aboard the famous Fletliner trains, named after the Fletton bricks produced there, although the name devices from an area of Peterborough, where the bricks were first made. In the 1930s a forest of 130 vast chimneys dominated the landscape round here. Even as recently as the 1970s, the county provided 20 per cent of Britain's bricks. But all that remains at Stewartby, where hundreds of workers would once bustle through its little station, are four giant chimneys preserved by English Heritage and the model dwellings constructed by the philanthropist owner Sir Malcolm Stewart for his workers. 'But watch those chimneys fall down now they've cooled after switching off the furnaces,' the conductor tells me, pressing his buzzer to start the train 'Be a good thing too – they're an eyesore. I'll tell you an interesting fact: they're planning to build the world's largest aquarium here one day soon. It'll be much better. We might get a few passengers along then.'

While most parts of south-east England are turning from green to brown as creeping suburbia takes over, the opposite is happening here, and the reason can be found in the slow march of vegetation across the acres once scarred by decades of clay extraction, brick making and landfill. Where dark satanic kilns and furnaces once stood, the clock has been turned back to a more bucolic age, and the ghosts of the old industries have fluttered away on the breeze. I walk on the path by the lineside between Stewartby and Millbrook stations in an area where a million new trees have been planted. Hares scamper away and there is the occasional bleat of a sheep. Young oaks are putting down their roots through the clay and brick dust, and the flowers of early summer are back as though they never went away. Here are creamy clouds of meadowsweet and the purple flowers of tufted vetch weaving their way through the hedgerows. There is the faint smell of wild basil from the railway embankment.

So hypnotically tranquil is it here, in the heat of midday, that it seems unsettling to discover another person. On Millbrook platform there is a man taking photographs. He introduces himself as Chris Toyer and tells me he has just retired after twenty-four years as a charge nurse in the accident and emergency unit at the Luton and Dunstable Hospital. It is possibly one of the most stressful places in the world, he explains, because it is so close to the M1 motorway and treats many acccident victims. 'I like to hang around on a quiet railway line like this,' he tells me, 'because you can get away from it all. The great thing about this line is that it's close to the local towns but in the middle of the countryside too. I remember as a boy walking along the old Luton–Dunstable line, now closed. Heading down the embankment I felt free of care.' I know exactly what he means. Brian Hollingsworth put it eloquently in his book *The Pleasures of Railways*: 'The world is somehow quite unselfconscious about being looked at from a railway . . .'

But Chris and I are not the only ones surveying the world from the trackside. In what was once the stationmaster's house on the platform is a bearded man in a rugby shirt busy making a mid-morning pot of coffee. He is David Thomas, who tells me he bought the house in 1984 – a snip, since this lovely half-timbered Victorian Gothic building with its elaborate bargeboards is one of the most handsome country railway stations to be found anywhere, in a style dictated by the dukes of Bedford, who weren't having any mediocre railway buildings on their estate. 'The place had been empty for twelve years and was in a pretty bad way. I decided to take it on with my family. The reason nobody had bought it was because it had a very small garden.' Since then, he's been able to buy the goods yard – all two and a half acres of it – and has raised his three teenage children in the station.

'I didn't buy it because I was a trainspotter,' he protests, though the kitchen table where we sit and have coffee is piled high with excursion handbills, tickets and black-and-white photographs from the steam days. 'What I really love is the local history,' he tells me, which he's had plenty of time to pursue since taking redundancy from his job as a banker at London's Canary Wharf. 'I've done lots of research and a large archive of paperwork about the line. Almost everything that's been published on the railway. I've got the entire story in my house here, the whole of its 164-year history.

'Look at this!' He rummages in one of his piles of memorabilia and pulls out a little card booklet, neatly printed in blue with a charming woodcut of a steam locomotive. It is headed 'Oxford University Railway Society, Trinity Term 1952. Rev. G. C. Stead (Keble), President'. The Reverend Stead is pleased to announce a visit of the Society to the Cambridge Union Railway Club on Saturday 7 June. 'Sums up the story of the line, doesn't it?' David says.

'I know some people who live in stations don't like the public very much, but I'm the opposite. We do get some coming here still asking for tickets, but I'm always friendly. I do open days here and invite people round and have events in the garden. We have stalls, bands playing, face painting. I've got some noticeboards I'm going to put up telling the history of the line. Do you know, when Network Rail modernised the old signalling six years ago the wreckers came round and smashed everything up? They preferred to do that than let people buy stuff. But I got a station name board and the old signaller's cabin. As for the future of the line, you've got to be realistic. There's only so much demand. But there are no trains on Sunday, and it would be nice to be able to get back of an evening from Bedford. The last train goes before 10 p.m. So everyone just uses their car instead, driving to and fro parallel to the line. It's madness.'

As he says goodbye, David's faith in his railway reminds me of the scene in the Ealing comedy *The Titfield Thunderbolt* in which a group of villagers is trying to save the local line. One character says, 'The Canterbury and Whitstable Line could not avoid closure.' 'Ah,' rejoins the other,' perhaps there were not men of sufficient faith in Canterbury.' Ever optimistic, David leads me through the old goods yard, across smooth lawns where track once rusted away, past the ancient guards van he has bought for the garden, past the goods shed, past his geese and past the hives where the buzzing of bees has replaced the bang and clatter of wagons. 'Sure we've lost the Oxford to Cambridge trains and in that sense the line is less than it was then. But do you know we've got more stations now than when the present line opened 164 years ago? There aren't many country railways where you can say that.'

And he is right. The Marston Vale Line is the perfect pocket-sized railway. It is possible to get off at every station, linger among the local charms and still arrive at your destination by the end of the day. After a few miles the train trundles into Lidlington, one of the few stations along the line that doesn't appear to be in the midst of a rural nowhere. Ignore the boxy little modern houses that have been built over the goods yard and follow the signs for the Greensand Ridge, which offers a forty-mile walk over the hills into Cambridgeshire. The steep slope on the edge of the village is reckoned to have been the inspiration for John Bunyan's Hill of Difficulty. As I slog up, I don't notice any chained lions, nor do I have to don my armour and joust with the Devil, but I can see why this sandy ridge played for Bunyan the part of the Delectable Mountains so perfectly. Here are gently rolling hills and tiny valleys, with pockets of woodland where it is possible to disturb adders and green tiger beetles under your feet. Old pollard willows and native black poplars line the banks of the Rivers Flit and Ouzel, which sound as though they belong to the magical world of *Down the Bright Stream*, the 1950s novel about the countryside by the writer BB, whose other book, *The Forest of Bowland Light Railway*, has also delighted generations of young children fascinated by trains.

Heading west the train has to climb a delectable mountain of its own, the famous Brogborough Bank, where in steam days photographers would gather to capture images of perspiring locomotives shooting towering clouds of steam into the sky as they climbed the 1 in 105 gradient. From the summit it is possible to see across the whole of Bedfordshire and the Celestial City of Bedford itself. One day boats as well as trains may be soon be labouring up here, since there are plans to open a branch of the Grand Union Canal to Bedford with a special spiral boat lift to get them over the hill.

Like Millbrook, Ridgmont has a handsome station building, but it appears to be derelict. However, inside, among the rot and weeds I discover another devotee of the Marston Vale Line. Stephen Sleight, an owlish and serious young man with a degree in tourism from the University of Gloucestershire, is the line's community rail partnership officer. He tells me he has been given a lease by Network Rail to refurbish the station as a museum of railway history. He also provides me with a reminder that I need to keep on the straight and narrow on my Bunyan pilgrimage, since by coincidence he turns out to be a regular worshipper at Bunyan's famous church, the Bunyan Meeting back in Bedford. The decor in the Ridgmont stationmaster's house is just as it was when last occupied by the former crossing keeper, with Festival of Britain wallpaper in the living room and peeling yellow Fablon in the kitchen. Stephen shows me the old booking office: 'Look, there's the ticket hatch used by the booking clerk.' Grass is growing high through the floor of the gents and, most poignant of all, painted on the windowsill are handwritten instructions, specifying how long to hold open the crossing gates, depending on whether a goods or a passenger train was passing.

Stephen is delighted with a pile of rusting signs from the stations on the line, donated by Silverlink Trains after that company's franchise came to an end in 2007 in favour of London Midland. (Why do train companies forced to operate lines such as this on a shoestring spend fortunes on branding exercises? Do often absurd-sounding company names created by focus groups sell tickets any better than plain old British Railways?)

The old wooden level-crossing gates went for scrap in 2004. Until then, Stephen tells me, not much had changed in this backwater. The signalling, with its wooden signal boxes, rustling wires, semaphore arms and clanking levers, was thrown out at the same time. The Bedford Historical Record Society, meanwhile, has a delightful account of the journey of one Mr Wade-Gery along the line in 1847:

> He would arrive at St Johns station by horse-drawn vehicle and wait while his paper ticket was written out. From the low platform, it would be quite a step up into the four-wheeled vehicle, lighted, if first class, by an oil lamp. This was a November day, but there would be no heating in the carriage. At the head of the train would be a diminutive 'Bury' engine, which would jerk the train into motion, as all the carriages were loose-coupled. The short coaches would clatter over the wrought-iron rails, which, only 20 feet in length, would give a bumpy ride. The stop at the station would be effected by the fireman and guard each screwing down a hand brake. The loose-fitted coaches would come together, the shock being diminished by buffers stuffed with horsehair. If the line into Bletchley was not clear, a policeman with frock coat and top hat would signal to the driver to stop.

The present-day technology on the line could not be more mundane. The signalling for the entire route is controlled from a grey, windowless, air-conditioned box on the opposite side of the tracks merging in style and period with the vast Amazon book warehouse next door – another modern megalith which towers over the surrounding fields. The Amazon model of goods delivery, some might argue, is the logical extension of Beeching's philosophy. Just as the BR chairman shut down all those little goods yards and sidings in favour of centralised freight distribution, so today's small independent bookshops find themselves too often in the literary equivalent of a weed-covered siding, outpaced and outpriced by Amazon. Some 15 per cent of all books bought in Britain are sourced through Ridgmont, including, quite possibly, the one that you have in your hand. But, Stephen tells me, commuting Amazon staff provide the line with a handy source of revenue. Ridgmont is famous otherwise as the birthplace of Cecilia Bowes-Lyon, Countess of Strathmore and Kinghome, mother of the late Queen Mother, and as the closest station to Woburn Safari Park, although this is not of much use to train passengers who don't want to be eaten, since access to the park is only permitted to visitors in cars.

It's just a short hop from here to the next station, which could not be more aptly named since Aspley Guise provided cover for one of the most top-secret operations of the Second World War. In Church Street, a short walk from the station, behind closed wrought iron gates is The Rookery, an anonymous red-brick house which was the headquarters of the Psychological War Executive, whose job it was to demoralise the populations of the Axis countries. From behind the anonymous curtains of The Rookery, black propaganda was beamed to Germany, as well as radio programmes to occupied Europe. Did you know that Hitler had Jewish ancestry? You could have found out by tuning into the broadcasts of Berlin-born Australian Denis Sefton Delmer. He knew Hitler personally and had lived in Germany before the war. According to the book *Spy Capital of Britain* by the appropriately named Stephen Bunker, the German for rookery is *Krahenhorst*, which also translates as 'den of thieves'. Delmer later became chief foreign correspondent of the *Daily Express*, where he deployed a different set of propagandist's skills on behalf of his boss Lord Beaverbrook.

I have been warned not to alight at the next station, Woburn

Sands, expecting to find a beach – as apparently many passengers have done over the years, even bringing buckets and spades. But where better to stop for lunch than the Station Hotel, a worn but inviting-looking Victorian boozer, painted in that maroon and cream livery that many pubs once wore, giving them the appearance of a 1950s railway station. It seems as though Kevin the landlord might be a bit of a railway buff, since the wall of the bar is lined with railway artefacts, including a reproduction nameplate from a Southern Railway King Arthur locomotive. But I am baffled by his painted inn sign outside, which depicts a Great Western Railway Prairie tank letting off steam beside the platform at Woburn Sands. Every trainspotter knows this is unlikely ever to have happened, and trainspotters hate inaccuracy with a vehemence only exceeded by their loathing of Jeremy Clarkson.

'The truth is, I know nothing about trains,' Kevin informs me, leaning across the bar in the way that pub landlords do when they are commencing a bit of a lecture. 'See that painting over there?' He points to a picture of the same engine but in a very Great Western scene, in a rustic part of the West Country. 'I got that at auction twenty-four years ago when I went to bid for a wardrobe. That's where I got the idea for my sign from. I couldn't care less if it's wrong.' But I suspect that Kevin secretly loves the Marston Vale Line with a passion equal to that of David Thomas and Stephen Sleight. 'When they tore down the signalling,' he confides, 'I got some of the signals, the levers from the signal box and even the relays' – which I notice he has ranged carefully around the top of the bar – 'and,' he says triumphantly, 'I even got the old sign with the Woburn Sands name on it.'

But through the window of the bar I can already spy the next train coming, which takes me on to Bow Brickhill, famous through the centuries for Bow Brickhill Steamed Pudding. As we reach Fenny Stratford, the line switches back to single track and then crosses Fenny Lock on the Grand Union Canal, from where it is possible to take scenic walks south to Leighton Buzzard and north to Milton Keynes. The afternoon drinkers are already clustered around the Red Lion pub on the towpath. Depending on levels of sobriety, it is possible to operate the manual swing bridge that crosses the canal. Motor buffs might note that Fenny is the place where the heavy oil engine was invented, and there is a plaque on the side of the Foundry Pub in Denmark Street commemorating its inventor Herbert Akroyd Stuart. Sadly we cannot truly describe it as a diesel engine – even though that is what it was – since Rudolf Diesel was triumphant in a patent dispute between the two men. Nice to know, though, that this marvel of the modern age, which propels the train on which we are travelling today, was really invented by a Brit.

Our single-coach train is dwarfed as it sneaks around the back of Bletchley station and through the carriage sidings, as if feeling slightly ashamed to mingle with all the grand expresses on the main line. Bletchley is a dispiriting place which appears to have had the life sucked out of it by neighbouring Milton Keynes. So don't turn left out of the station, where you will find only a soulless and half-tenanted 1980s shopping mall and a high street dominated by pound shops – and, for some reason, a disproportionate number of butchers'. Instead, cross the road and turn into the drive of Bletchley Park, the world's first large-scale code-breaking centre, where the Cambridge mathematician Alan Turing and the cream of Oxbridge's academics raced against time to crack Germany's Enigma code. 'Bletchley Park was Britain's greatest achievement of 1939–45 and perhaps the twentieth century,' wrote George Steiner, the cultural historian. And there can be few other buildings where a connection with the railways has played such a major part in the security of the nation.

The house and surrounding huts, which once accommodated more than 8,000 people, have an authentically melancholy 1940s atmosphere on this dark and drizzly afternoon. It had previously been the splendid country estate of a Victorian stockbroker, Herbert Samuel Leon, who bought the house because it was handily situated just across the road from Bletchley station and thus convenient for his London office. When his family put it up for sale on his death, the War Department snapped it up for a similar reason – it was opposite a railway station midway between Oxford and Cambridge Universities. Taking the train were legions of the brightest intellectuals in the land. Here was J R R Tolkien, from Oxford, slightly shambling, with Hobbits on his mind, probably seeking out a smoking compartment so he could puff on his pipe. Heading in the other direction on the Cambridge train was the young Dr Turing, dapper and dashing.

Back at the station, the clouds have cleared and the evening sun is glowing behind the vast concrete railway flyover, built in the 1960s, on which the line once continued through Buckinghamshire and on to Oxford's dreaming spires. There are plans, if sufficient money can be found, to reopen this section under a grand scheme known as East–West Rail. A short stub at the Oxford end, reviving the service from Bicester, has already reopened and is destined to form part of a bold new route to take trains from Oxford into London's Marylebone station. In the meantime, the tracks continue to rust and the grass and buddleia grow high amid the sleepers. Only memories remain. In days gone by, the Reverend Stead might already have ordered the cucumber sandwiches and poured the sherry in his rooms at Keble College in anticipation of the arrival of the distinguished members of the Cambridge Union Railway Club on the midday train. Talk of the old days of steam and long-closed wayside halts with pretty names such as Wootton Pillinge, Marsh Gibbon and Gamlingay would have gone on long into the evening until the sun set over the Isis and the last Brain Train was sounding its hooter ready to depart homewards to the Fens.

Enjoy the magnificent scenery of the **RHEIDOL VALLEY** from the miniature trains on British Railways' only narrow gauge passenger line. No visit to Aberystwyth is complete without seeing Devil's Bridge.

CHEAP DAY TICKETS

EVERY DAY BY ANY TRAIN

RETURN **2/9** FARE

TRAIN SERVICE			WEEKDAYS 13th June to 17th September SUNDAYS 24th July to 28th August			
			SATS. EXCEPTED			SUNDAYS ONLY
ABERYSTWYTH	dep	10.15 a.m.	1.45 p.m.	2.30 p.m.	5.45 p.m.	2.15 p.m.
LLANBADARN	dep	10.22 a.m.	1.52 p.m.	2.37 p.m.	5.52 p.m.	2.22 p.m.
DEVIL'S BRIDGE	arr	11.15 a.m.	2.45 p.m.	3.30 p.m.	6.45 p.m.	3.15 p.m.
			SATS. EXCEPTED		†	SUNDAYS ONLY
DEVIL'S BRIDGE	dep	11.45 a.m.	4.15 p.m.	5.50 p.m.	8.0 p.m.	4.30 p.m.
LLANBADARN	arr	12.39 p.m.	5.9 p.m.	6.45 p.m.	8.55 p.m.	5.24 p.m.
ABERYSTWYTH	arr	12.45 p.m.	5.15 p.m.	6.50 p.m.	9.0 p.m.	5.30 p.m.

† Tuesdays, Wednesdays and Thursdays, 19th July to 25th August

Children under Three years of age, Free ; Three and under fourteen years of age, Half-fare

SPECIAL CHEAP EVENING TICKETS

Tuesdays, Wednesdays and Thursdays, 19th July to 25th August

RETURN **2/-** FARE

BRITISH RAILWAYS

Wales's wild west: The narrow-gauge Vale of Rheidol railway climbs 700 feet over 11 miles from Aberystwyth to Devil's Bridge in Ceredigion. It is one of the treats accessible from the Cambrian Line, which hugs the shores of Cardigan Bay, offering one of the world's most dramatic coastal rail rides.

CHAPTER SIX

THE 10.43 TO THE LONELIEST STATION – ALONG THE BANKS OF THE LOVELY DOVEY INTO WILD WEST WALES

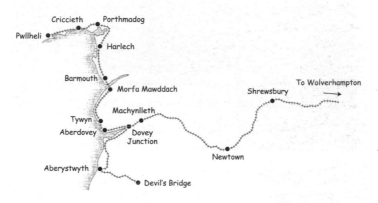

Wolverhampton to Aberystwyth and Pwllheli, via Newtown, Machynlleth, Dovey Junction, Aberystwyth, Aberdovey, Tywyn, Morfa Mawddach, Harlech, Porthmadog and Criccieth

Can there be a railway station more surreal in its function yet more beautiful in its setting anywhere in the world than Dovey Junction? I'm here to change trains at this lonely spot on the shores of Cardigan Bay – where the Cambrian Line to Aberystwyth and Pwllheli divides to run along both banks of the beautiful Dovey estuary – with just a couple of buffalo and a pair of ospreys for company.

Once, this empty platform in the middle of a marsh, with just a rudimentary shelter and half a mile of deserted tarmac and no obvious habitation nearby, had an important role as the place where travellers along the coast from north to south

Wales changed trains to cross the broad estuary, whose shifting sands between Ynys Las and Aberdovey had defeated even the most audacious of Victorian bridge builders. At this station were once one of the biggest waiting rooms in the country and an impressive signal box controlling an array of semaphores. The old refreshment room windows were frequently misted up with steam from sizzling urns as passengers queued for strong tea and Welsh cakes to fortify them for the rest of what was, and still is, one of the slowest and remotest journeys in Britain. Nowadays there are just butterflies, the sound of wind rustling in the grasses, the cinnamon scent of the bog myrtle and the breakers on the shore, not far distant.

These days too the timetable means it's generally easier to change, if you are travelling from Pwllheli to Aberystwyth, at the more commodious station one stop back in the hospitable town of Machynlleth. But windswept Dovey Junction is still there, standing lonely sentry at the point where the old counties of Montgomery, Merioneth and Cardigan meet. The station has even entered modern popular culture, with a song to be found on YouTube, performed by a student band from Aberystwyth University, called 'What's the Function of Dovey Junction?':

> What's the function of Dovey Junction?
> Standing alone, no telephone.
> Nowhere to go
> But straight back to you.

'Why do you want to get off at Dovey?' asks the conductor as I give him notice to halt the train to let me alight. ('Calls on request. Passengers wishing to leave the train must inform the guard and those wishing to join must give a hand signal to the driver,' it says in the timetable.) It seems an odd question for one whose job it is to sell tickets, but I suppose he's worried that I've made a mistake. 'Well, there are the ospreys,' I venture defensively, feeling slightly embarrassed at stopping the train just for me. There has been much excitement since a pair of rare breeding ospreys nested at the end of the platform, which is in the heart of the Dyfi nature reserve. 'That's as may be,' the conductor harrumphs, 'but *he*'s buggered off and hasn't been seen this year and left *her* holding the babies – that is if there are any.' But one of the passengers interjects, for this is a train in the heart of rural Wales, where friendliness is the default, 'No, it's lovely there. One of the top ten romantic places in Britain.' She explains that her name is Sue and she is a psychotherapist from Aberystwyth. 'Sometimes we come up from town of an evening with a bottle of wine and some nibbles, and just gaze at the stars.'

I discover, as I step off the train, that Dovey Junction is if anything more beautiful still in the solitude of the heat of the day. Out at sea the wind is churning up white breakers capping a deep-blue ocean. Could that be a seal or a porpoise out there riding the waves? Certainly, there are plenty of both creatures usually to be seen here, chasing the mackerel up to the shore. And then these are salt-marsh sheep, grazing the tasty spartina grasses, samphire, sea lavender and thrift, which give the meat a delicious sweet flavour. (Rick Stein cooked Welsh salt-marsh lamb at a Downing Street banquet when the French president came to stay.) Could it be a mirage when I spot some water buffalo shuffling along at the end of the platform? No. Like the ospreys, they too seem to have found refuge at this remote station on the idyllic fringe of the world.

The sun was already high in the sky as I had set off west that morning out of Wolverhampton's bland modern station on a packed four-coach train. True, our Class 158 diesel multiple unit had a rather jolly swirly carpet that suggested it might be more than just a commuter train, but otherwise this could be any mundane suburban journey through the west Midlands. Like many 158s around the country, this unrefurbished train dating from British Rail days has a problem with its air conditioning, and the tiny windows are open as wide as can be. People are snoozing everywhere. But who cares, with the prospect of one of the most ravishingly beautiful journeys in Europe along the tracks ahead. Unusually for a modern train, there are 1950s-style paper stickers on the window announcing its destination (*Gorsafoedd i*/Stations to Pwllheli), as though somehow the British Railways Western Region is still alive and thinks it is running the Cambrian Coast Express, which used to be a regular on this line. With its chocolate and cream coaches loaded with bucket-and-spade families off on their holidays and a plucky little Brunswick-green 4-6-0 Manor Class locomotive, or even an elderly Dukedog on the front, the 11.10 Cambrian Coast Express from Paddington was possibly the most evocative and glamorous named train ever to run on a long-distance single track railway.

Ahead on the Cambrian Line, we have exactly the same prospect as those excited post-war families, as we travel over mile after mile of single line over switchback gradients, with few passing places, into one of the most sensationally beautiful river estuaries in Britain. This is a journey that will take us into dramatic mountains and echoing valleys, through landscapes etched with historic struggles, past busy seaside resorts and tiny coastal villages on the edge of vast sandy beaches with glimpses of ruined castles and abbeys, passing ancient hill forts with views across ocean and hills.

Perhaps nobody could have put it better than the general manager of the old Cambrian Railways company himself, on a poster that used to adorn the stations:

> The scenery traversed by and adjacent to the Cambrian
> Railways is of an exceedingly varied and beautiful
> description; and the coast of Cardigan Bay, to which the
> line affords the most convenient access, offers great
> advantages for sea-bathing in the long reaches of firm, safe,

and sandy beach with which it abounds and in its pure and bracing air . . . New corridor coaches lighted with gas. Signed C. S. DENNISS [who was clearly fond of spelling his name with capital letters], Secretary and General Manager, Cambrian Railways, Oswestry.

By the time we get to Shrewsbury, the suits with laptops and the shoppers have mostly vanished, and the train starts to take on a jolly seaside atmosphere in anticipation of the journey to the coast ahead. 'I'm afraid we'll have to wait twenty minutes here,' announces Iorwerth, the conductor. 'We're going to have to stop for a late 'un coming up the line.' Iorwerth ('Call me Iorwy') says that until recently the line had one of the worst lateness records of any in Britain because of the difficulties in getting trains past each other over long stretches of single track. 'It's getting better. But it's not that good now – just you wait and see.' As we finally crawl out of Shrewsbury underneath the vast signal box at Severn Bridge Junction, the largest surviving mechanical signal box in Europe with 180 levers, all still pulled by hand, he points out some old yellow diesel locos with big American style noses by the line-side. ' Built by craftsmen at English Electric they were.' I ask him: aren't all Welshmen supposed to look down on everything English? 'Ah, but this was quality. Half a century old, these lovely old dears. They used to be called the D6700s but now they're called Class 97s. That's because they're kitted out with equipment to test our new signalling system. Can you believe it? This old Cambrian Railways line is going to be the most modern in Britain.'

He explains that the tracks we're about to travel on are the first in Britain to operate the techie-sounding European Rail Traffic Management System – ERTMS as it is called. 'Sounds complicated,' he tells me. 'But don't you worry. It means that we can do away with signals altogether and the trains can run with a computer in the cab, making sure that we can get up real close to the train in front without crashing into it. Only the Eurostars can do that on the main line. Not that I'm any fan of the Frenchies, mind you!'

I think of this as our train clanks across the points when we switch onto the long single track of the Cambrian Line at the old signal box at Sutton Bridge Junction, peeling away from the main line south to Newport. Here, as far back as anyone can remember, the signalman would lean out to hand over a metal token in a leather harness to the 'driver in possession'. Since the 1980s the handover has been done virtually via a radio link between the driver and the signal box. But this too in the digital era is now dinosaur analogue technology. I speculate that Britain's greatest railway engineer, Isambard Kingdom Brunel, would have been thrilled with this state-of-the-art stuff, since he was a fan of single-track railways. Back in 1852 he wrote, 'It is now universally admitted that when a single object is to be attained, arrangements may easily be made by which a short length of single line can be worked without any inconvenience.' But he was commenting on the track over his famous Saltash Bridge from Devon into Cornwall. Since then the bridge has become one of the famous bottlenecks on the national system. Could a genius be wrong? Well, yes, sometimes.

We're picking up speed, rattling along past the 2,000-year-old Bredon Hill fort, just after which we will cross the Welsh border. Already along the train you can hear the lilt of Welsh being spoken. The local people rejoice in it, for this is Europe's oldest living language. Iorwerth is in chatty mood. 'Did you know,' he says, resting against a seat, 'that there are three times as many sheep as people in Wales? Or that Wales has fewer miles of electrified track than any country in Europe except Albania?' Here now is the line of Offa's Dyke, the 177-mile earth bank and ditch along the Welsh border, dug in the eighth century to protect the kingdom of Mercia, now the English Midlands, from Welsh marauders. Soon the Shropshire Union Canal comes in from the north, sinewing alongside the tracks.

When the railway was built in the 1860s, the horses pulling the barges faced redundancy, but it took until 1935 before the canal was finally abandoned to the weeds. Now it has a new future and is being restored to navigable standards.

The railways into this part of Wales took the best part of a century to supersede the tried and trusted canals, and had their origins in a fantasy line called the Manchester and Milford, whose backers dreamed rosy dreams of freight coming this way from industrial Lancashire to the port of Milford Haven in west Wales. It came to very little, and as historian L T C. Rolt observes in his book *Lines of Character*, 'The railway promoters stood on the Marches of Wales like the advance guard of an invading army, probing the enemy's defences . . . which the mountains defeated as they defeated the invading armies of the past. From Shrewsbury and Craven Arms . . . they set out confidently westwards only to waver and fall back like the ruled roads of the Romans before them.'

But along came a bold engineer called David Davies, who carved this line through Newtown to the coast. It climbs 373 feet from Caersws to its summit and falls a spectacular 645 feet to the level of the Dovey at Machynlleth, with no gradient steeper than 1 in 52. No wonder Davies became Wales's first self-made millionaire. As Rolt put it, 'In his pride, Davies scorned to burrow under his native mountains but chose to carve them like a sculptor, despite the additional work involved.' At the summit of Talerddig, where it passes through a defile 120 feet deep, the line is hewn through the solid rock, which makes a more impressive gateway to west Wales than any tunnel.

In the end, out of the complicated railway politics of the era the Cambrian Railways Company was formed. This was an entirely Welsh enterprise composed of various smaller lines – the Oswestry and Newtown, the Newtown and Machynlleth, the Aberystwyth and Welsh Coast, the Oswestry, Ellesmere and Whitchurch, the Wrexham and Ellesmere and the Mid

Wales — that gave, in the words of one Cambrian historian, 'two fingers to the English' until the whole caboodle fell into the hands of the Great Western Railway at Paddington in 1923. Even today it is not hard to find signs of the old Cambrian heritage along the line. At Caersws the signal box in original Cambrian Railways colours still survives, controlling the level crossings as it did when the poet John Ceiriog Hughes, the 'Robert Burns of Wales', was stationmaster here. The old station at Talerddig has gone, but the stationmaster's house lives on as a private residence — and very smart it is too. There is plenty of time to admire it, since we are halted, engines idling, yet again to let another late train pass on the loop.

At Machynlleth the severe-looking but commodious stone station buildings are unchanged since the Cambrian Railways era, but thank goodness for that. The waiting room is inviting and the ticket office is still staffed and functioning. Iorwerth is scurrying down the train making sure passengers are in the right two carriages before it splits and he hands over to new crews. Oh, Mr Porter! You don't want to be carried on to Pwllheli if you're planning to travel to Aberystwyth. It could take you a day to get back. For me it doesn't matter since I shall soon be away with the ospreys and buffalo at Dovey Junction. But thereafter I must return to my schedule, since I have an appointment with a special narrow-gauge train at Aberystwyth.

One of the joys of the Cambrian Line is that it provides connections with a charming ragbag of steam narrow-gauge railways mostly dating back to the time when slate was mined in these parts. Nowhere in the world is it possible to change trains over such a short distance onto so many lines which have played such an intimate part in the industrial archaeology of a nation. In the port of Tywyn you can hop onto the Talyllyn Railway, the first volunteer-run narrow-gauge railway in the world and made famous by the Reverend Awdry as the fictional Skarloey Railway in his book *Four Little Engines*. Its bigger brother the Ffestiniog climbs thirteen and a half miles from

Porthmadog on the coast, past lakes and waterfalls, through sensational horseshoe bends into the mountains at Blaenau Ffestiniog, to claim its own distinction as the world's oldest independent railway company. Longer still is the Welsh Highland Railway, which, when its latest extension is fully operational, will snake through the Snowdonia National Park for twenty-two miles as far as Caernarfon. If this isn't enough, you may take your pick from the Llanberis Lake Railway, the Snowdon Mountain Railway, the Bala Lake Railway, the Welshpool and Llanfair Railway and the Brecon Mountain Railway.

This afternoon I've chosen the Vale of Rheidol Railway, whose little 1-foot-11¾-inch-gauge engines climb 700 feet up the eleven miles to Devil's Bridge. The line had a special place in the heart of every 1960s schoolboy as the home of the last steam engines in regular service on the nationalised network. How ironic that as other secondary lines across Wales were being slaughtered by Beeching, the little Vale of Rheidol lived on. Now operated privately, No. 7 *Owain Glyndwr*, No. 8 *Llywelyn* and No. 9 *Prince of Wales* have outlasted their larger sisters by more than forty years to become the last continuously operating remnant of British Rail steam. They even survived the indignity of being painted like bog-standard diesels, complete with modern double arrow logo, when British Rail went through its Stalinist phase of painting everything in sight drab 'rail blue' in the early 1970s.

Today *Llywelyn* is all spit and polish in gleaming Great Western green as it tugs its hard-seated wooden carriages out of the old Carmarthen platform at Aberystwyth, twisting and turning as it puffs up gradients of nearly 1 in 50. No wonder that speeds only average 12 mph, and often slower if the rails are wet. It would be tempting to linger at Devil's Bridge and scramble down the pathways to the foaming whirlpool called the Devil's Punchbowl, but already the sun is starting to dim and *Llywelyn* is running round its carriages for the last return journey of the day. At Aberystwyth there's just time to dunk my toes in the sea, along with the students from the university swigging from bottles of Tesco Chardonnay as they celebrate completing their finals. Where better for an evening meal, as I wait for the last train back to Machynlleth, than in the Aberystwyth station buffet? I am to stay the night at the White Lion, an old coaching inn in Machynlleth. 'It has impeccable railway connections,' says Iorwerth. 'Wendy the manageress is engaged to one of the drivers. And we hold our RMT meetings there.'

Rather like the famous marketing slogan for the Victoria and Albert Museum in London, the handsome stone buildings of Aberystwyth station could now be described as 'a pub with a station attached'. WETHERSPOON'S, YR HEN ORSAF, it says across the front of the building where the sign for the Great Western Railway might once have hung proudly. 'What does *Yr Hen Orsaf* mean?' I ask the barman, who looks at me as though I am an alien. 'Why, the Old Railway Station of course.' On the concourse, where passengers arriving on the Cambrian Coast Express might have paused with their suitcases before heading for their fortnight's stay at Mrs Thomas's and Mrs Jenkins' boarding houses are tables full of people on an evening out, slugging cheap wine and munching on 'Beer 'n' a Burger' promotions. But after a pint of two of Felinfoel Double Dragon, who cares if the train is late?

Waking up in Machynlleth next morning, what had seemed a severe little town, watched over by its 'bible-black' chapels straight out of *Under Milk Wood,* has taken on a more colourful hue. The surrounding fields are a brilliant Pre-Raphaelite green and the river is frosted-glass-sparkly as though in a model railway. The station too is like an idealised country junction straight out of a train-set wrapping, with a little signal box to pull the semaphore signals controlling the sidings. It still has its old stone-built steam shed, which forms part of a new £3 million complex where today's diesel trains are maintained. This features a large sign reading MACHYNLLETH TRAIN CARE.

(Where do the trains go to sleep at night, Daddy? In the Train Care, Darling.)

I'm taking the 09.03 to Pwllheli, the first service of the day to arrive from the West Midlands, which will traverse what is known as the Coast Line along the north side of the estuary. The Class 158 has already come 110 miles from Wolverhampton, and there are another two hours and twenty-six stations to go before we reach our destination. 'Mr Williams, is it?' asks the booking clerk, a smiling young woman called Mo Kohler. She has remembered me from booking a ticket the day before. This is Welsh country charm at its best. At Machynlleth everyone is made to feel important.

As we head north along the coast through Aberdovey I get chatting to Gus, who tells me he is the train's rubbish collector – 'Train Presentation Team', it says on his T-shirt – though it is clear his expertise is in the history and topography of the line rather than discarded sandwich wrappings. 'I'm actually a Scouser,' he tells me, 'but my mother still lives on that hill over there.' And he provides a continuous commentary as the train crawls along the coast. Aberdyfi is the first ever Outward Bound Centre, founded in 1941. Inland at Tywyn is the outline of Craig yr Aderyn (Bird Rock), once a sea cliff where the cormorants still nest even though the sea is several miles away. We pull into Llwyngwril – 'Squirrel, many people call it,' says Gus. 'It's actually spoken Lo-in-goo-ril, but however you pronounce it you will find a Welshman to correct you. It's a curious fact that it's the only station with the letters GWR incorporated in its name.'

An imposing woman dressed all in black emerges from the station building, which is now a private house, and climbs aboard. She introduces herself as Margaret Bridges, whose husband was once general manager of the line. 'Very impressive lady,' says Gus, and there's a bit of a deferential hush round the carriage. It's clear that old social hierarchies still live on in this part of rural west Wales.

Now we're in for a spectacular ride along the cliff tops. There are few railways anywhere in Europe that can compete with this. The train climbs steadily, hugging the shoreline, passes gingerly over a foaming waterfall and slows to walking pace before passing onto a narrow cliff edge one hundred feet above the foaming breakers of Cardigan Bay. The seagulls, solicitous for their young in the clifftop nests, wheel and cry around the carriage windows. Once there was a spectacular accident here. The journalist Alexander Frater describes it in his book *Stopping Train Britain*:

> Soon afterwards the line began its cautious approach to the Friog, the notorious section where it runs along a ledge cut into the side of a cliff. It was here, on March 4 1933, that a rock fall caused the engine of the early morning mail from Aberystwyth to spin off the rails and tumble onto the boulders a hundred feet below; its single carriage, a converted Dean clerestory with its dining alcoves and first class dog lockers removed for service along the coast, remained sitting intact on the track. When the rising tide began to lap around the tangled wreckage of the locomotive, the smallest railwayman in the salvage party, a ganger named W. A. Spoonley, was ordered to crawl into the crushed cab to extract the remains of the driver and fireman. The official with the green lamp, who had daily walked the line before the first train came through, and who had been fired as an economy measure, was promptly reinstated.

A concrete avalanche shelter was later installed here, which is still the only one of its kind in Britain.

There's more drama to come as the dark mass of Cader Idris rears above the train to the right, rising to 2,927 feet. The name means 'Chair of Idris the Giant', and legend says that whoever spends a night at the summit will return either a madman or a poet. But things are calming down now as we approach the Mawddach estuary and reach the little seaside resort of Fairbourne, with its miniature railway and views of Barmouth on the other side. We halt briefly at Morfa Mawddach where the ghosts of the old railway still haunt the platform, for this was once a grand rambling station known as Barmouth Junction. ('Change for Dolgellau, Bala, Ruabon and stations onwards into England' – though sadly no more since the entire line was liquidated by Beeching in 1965.) Now we are slowing again for the coast's most magnificent civil engineering feature, the half-mile-long Barmouth Bridge with its 113 timber spans and two extended steel ones, the longest timber trestle bridge in Wales. Lucky it is still here, because recently it was nearly lost to the ravages of nature. An attack by the toredo marine worm in 1980, which weakened the structure severely, nearly dealt the coast line the same fate as the old Dolgellau route. Lucky the money was found for repairs.

And so the little stations roll by as we crawl gently along the coast. At Llanaber the railway runs right by the beach, and passing through Llanbedr you can catch a glimpse of Shell Island, where the beaches are strewn with shells after winter storms and which houses the largest tent campsite in Europe. Just to keep your Welsh pronunciation up to scratch there's another 'Llan' – Llandanwg, where you can spot a thirteenth-century church in the dunes which sometimes has to be dug out of the sands after a storm. Past Harlech, with its great grim castle high on the rock next to the station, and Tygwyn, where you can spy the towers and domes of Portmeirion, Clough Williams-Ellis's fantasy Italianate village built between 1925 and 1975. The tiny halt at Landecwyn is so small it's possible only to open one door of the train.

At every station it's busy – so much so that two conductors, Louise and Dave, are needed to cope. 'It's just like a bus, this train,' Louise says. 'It's the only way people can get around.

Thank the Lord they never closed it.' Along the carriage an elderly farmer in a baseball cap with most of his teeth missing is telling the couple opposite that he is returning from a hospital appointment. 'I go for a check-up in Aberystwyth every twelve-month, see, and I pop in on the girlfriend on the way home,' he says with a leery wink. Through the windows the sea is as blue as can be, almost a caricature of those idealised GWR holiday posters of the 1930s.

All around me, as the train stops and starts in the midday heat, people are dozing. I think of Ian Fleming's description of James Bond nodding off in *Live and Let Die*, 'listening to the steady gallop of the wheels and the gentle rattles and squeaks in the coachwork that bring sleep on so quickly' – although if there is a Mr Big around this morning in this quiet corner of Wales, he is not readily apparent. We're on the fringes of Snowdonia now, passing Minffordd and Porthmadog, from where the little narrow-gauge line runs up to Blaenau Ffestiniog. The purple blooms of the rhododendrons appearing along the trackside may look charming, but this non-native plant is a pest, producing up to a million seeds from a single bush, and much money is spent every year uprooting them from the national park. Next station is Criccieth, home of David Lloyd George and where Robert Graves wrote 'Welsh Incident', his comic parody of rural Wales – famously performed by Richard Burton:

> The Harlech Silver Band played Marchog Jesu
> On thirty-seven shimmering instruments
> Collecting for Caernarvon's (Fever) Hospital Fund.
> The populations of Pwllheli, Criccieth,
> Portmadoc, Borth, Tremadoc, Penrhyndeudraeth,
> Were all assembled. Criccieth's mayor addressed them
> First in good Welsh and then in fluent English,
> Twisting his fingers in his chain of office,
> Welcoming the things. They came out on the sand . . .

After Pen y Chain, where thousands once alighted for the former Butlin's holiday camp and where Ringo Starr performed in pre-Beatles days, we are at journey's end at the buffer stops in Pwllheli, where there's just time to wolf down some cod and chips in the thirty minutes before the train returns south. Why is everyone in the chippy speaking Welsh? Obvious, really. Pwllheli is the spiritual centre of Welsh-speaking Wales, and this is where Plaid Cymru was founded in 1925.

As we pull into Harlech, travelling south again, it seems that there's a bit of a party going on. Here is a group of – well – ladies of a certain age, daubing brightly coloured pictures on the station shelter. They introduce themselves as Pat, Denise, Myfanwy, Edwina and Jan, all from the Women's Institute, and explain they are doing a mural 'to brighten the place up'. It certainly needs it – the old Cambrian Railways stationmaster's house on the opposite platform is boarded up and rotting and an affront to the breathtaking presence of King Edward I's mighty Harlech Castle towering above us. 'We're all WI ladies,' they explain. 'But don't call us Calendar Girls – it's a bit chilly round here for that kind of thing.' But Jan says, 'Oh, I don't know. We could pose in just our high vis jackets.' The artist in charge is a local student called Helen Jones, who claims, with a straight face, that she is more Banksy than Leonardo, and says that the outcome is to be a *Mabinogion*, a panorama of the ancient legends of Wales. 'I've never done a proper mural before. I once did one of a goldfish on my boyfriend's bedroom wall, but he left me soon afterwards.'

Looking on in bafflement is a gaunt old man who tells me his name is Rhys Evans, who was once signalman here. 'I retired in 1960, see, so you can guess how old I am now. We had proper trains then and the signal box was open all night for the freights that ran through – cattle, coal, explosives from the factory up at Penrhyndeudraeth. There were fourteen of us working at the station then; now look at the state of it, boy,' he says, pointing to the crumbling stationmaster's house. 'I remember so well the roaring fires we had in there once – flames leaping up the chimney.'

Master of ceremonies at this platform-fest is a handsome young man with a rugby player's build who announces himself as Gerwyn Jones, the railway development officer for the line. 'I do anything and everything to keep it going. The local authorities and the train operating company put money into a pot to pay my insubstantial wages and provide a budget for me to help keep it all functioning. I come from a family of railwaymen. My father was a fireman on this line in steam days. But he also worked up at Old Oak Common on the Castles and other express locos till Dr Beeching made him redundant. He helped me to love the railway – not in an evangelical way – but like him I think these local lines are very important.

'We've got passenger numbers going up at a faster rate than the national average. Funny enough, we do better when the weather's bad on this coast, since there are few indoor attractions round here. How many railways in Britain have a national park on one side and "miles of glorious sands", as the Great Western used to describe it, on the other? I'm from Cardiganshire, so I've got short arms and long pockets. I refer to the Cambrian as being two for the price of one, with one view on he way up and another on the way down.' There's a twinkle in his eye as he says, 'Did you hear the one about the American visitor who got off here at Harlech? He looked up and said, "What foresight! They built the castle next to the railway station!"'

Gerwyn joins me on the next train south, declaring that he's going to get off at Dovey Junction and cycle to his home in Talybont (now I finally see the function of Dovey Junction). We are on the 14.30, and all being well it will get me back to London in five hours and forty-six minutes, changing at Birmingham International. But Gerwyn's face drops as he takes a call on his mobile phone: 'There's been a bridge bash up at Newtown,' he tells me, looking anxious, since he had been reassuring me that punctuality on the line was improving. A lorry has run into the base of a bridge and all services have been halted until it is inspected. When we pull in at Machynlleth, there's a further trauma. A small boy has dropped his teddy bear between the platform and the train. 'Don't worry,' Lynn the conductor reassures the howling infant. 'Teddy's just having an adventure.' The driver crawls beneath the carriage, and there is applause all round from the assembled passengers on the platform when the hero emerges clutching the delinquent beast.

Back on the main line at Talerddig, the conductor announces that the train down from Birmingham is running twenty minute late, 'so we'll be forced to stop here until it arrives'. Could there be a remoter or more peaceful place to halt for a while? No roads, no people; the sheep are lethargic, and not even the leaves are rustling on this humid afternoon in the middle of the hills in the most peaceful countryside Britain can offer. Twenty minutes turn into forty, and forty turn into an hour 'Well, actually, we're on time,' says the conductor with devilish Welsh sophistry. 'It's just the others up the line that are late.' And then there's an announcement over the intercom of an even worse disaster. The refreshment trolley has lost a wheel and has had to be taken out of use.

But there's no point fretting. We are on the Planet of the Slow Train. As we wait and the afternoon draws on, engines beneath the carriage idling soporifically, I think of the old days – of the Cambrian Coast Express, which despite its name would sometimes run out of puff here after the little engine's Herculean 'I think, I can, I think I can' climb up the 1 in 52 bank from Llanbrynmair to Talerddig summit. And Ruskin's words come to mind: 'There was always more in the world than men could see, walked they ever so slowly; they will see it no better for going fast. The really precious things are thought and sight, not pace. It does a man no harm to go slow; for his glory is not all in going, but in being.'

Small but beautiful: The Brockenhurst to Lymington branch is one of the shortest on the network but is crammed with scenic delights. It was also England's last steam-operated branch line. Here Ivatt 2-6-2T No. 41224 approaches Lymington Junction in summer 1966.

CHAPTER SEVEN

THE 09.59 TO LYMINGTON – MIND THE DOORS ON THE SLOW TRAIN TO BRITAIN'S MOST PERFECT COASTAL TOWN

Brockenhurst to Lymington Town and Lymington Pier

HARK! Listen! One of the most familiar sounds of a British railway station has vanished from the landscape. So imperceptibly has it departed that many have not yet noticed. Some stations still resound to the echo of loudspeaker announcements, although nowadays these are more likely to be repetitious warnings about leaving luggage unattended or on the perils of boarding with the wrong ticket rather than useful information about the departure of the 4.50 from Paddington. And the hiss of steam, the shriek of a whistle and the clanking of buffers have long gone. But when did you last hear the *clunk-bang* of a train door being slammed shut? From the birth of the railways until the first years of the twenty-first century the cacophony of carriage doors being closed resonated across the railway landscape. In contrast to the Elgar-style symphony of a train puffing sedately along a branch line, the sound of a train in a station was more like the jarring staccato of a Stockhausen quintet. At a major terminus like London Bridge or Victoria, where the sound of slamming doors resonated off great arched roofs, rush hour could sound like a gun battle in the trenches.

Most of the old slam-door trains had disappeared from normal service by 2005, and who was sorry? The 'slammers' were draughty and dangerous – many a passenger, possibly lubricated by a pint too many of Old Thunder at the Station Arms, had opened a door by mistake and fallen out onto the track. Plots of station bookstall crime thrillers were sustained by tales of villains bundling their victims out of the doors onto the lines. Over-eager commuters racing for their office desks would knock over passengers waiting on platforms like ninepins as they swung open the doors before the train had come to a stop. Apart from the ageing diesel HSTs, whose hinged doors are still operated by passengers, but which close with a more sedate *kerr-umph*, the day of the slammer is now over. The swish of sliding doors rules, and the writ of the health and safety police runs across the land.

But wait. What's this I hear as I emerge from the London train onto the platform at this handsome country junction in the heart of the New Forest? There's the sound of blackbirds singing on this warm spring morning, high in the ancient trees around us, but there's also the unmistakable staccàto of a train door slamming. In the little loop line platform is a 3-CIG three-coach electric train named *Farringford* built in 1963, the year of the infamous Beeching Report, retired from its duties on express trains to Brighton and Portsmouth and serving out its final days shuttling up and down the five-and-a-half-mile branch line from Brockenhurst to Lymington. Anoraks will know that CIG stands for 'corridor express train running on the Brighton line', the Brighton route having the operating code IG. But those with an interest in a more conventional kind of history might enjoy the connection with *Farringford*'s other heritage.

Farringford was the Isle of Wight home of Alfred, Lord Tennyson, where the great man wrote much of his finest poetry and hosted the great and good of Victorian society, including Lewis Carroll, Charles Darwin, William Holman Hunt and Garibaldi.

Quite apart from the beauty of the New Forest setting and its sensational panoramas over the Lymington and Boldre Rivers and out into the estuary and the Solent, the Lymington branch is special in many ways. It is one of the shortest surviving branch lines on the national network (although the Stourbridge Junction to Stourbridge Town branch in Worcestershire is shorter at less than a quarter the length), and Dr Richard Beeching especially loved to cull short branch lines, which rarely made any money and were costly to operate. But the Lymington line had a trick up its sleeve, evading the wicked doctor's grasp because it connected to the ferry to Yarmouth on the Isle of Wight, an essential mainland link to the western end of the island.

The Lymington line was special too as the very last branch line in England to be operated by steam, retaining its little local engine until April 1967, only a year before steam on the national network finished altogether. No. 41312, which operated the final steam service, is still rattling away in Hampshire on the preserved Mid-Hants Railway. Today the line is also proud of its other distinguishing characteristic as one of the last remaining railways in Britain where passengers are transported by train along a pier to meet a ferry. Long gone are the days when loaded expresses from London disgorged passengers heading for Paris, Istanbul, Moscow and exotic points east at Folkestone Harbour or Dover Marine to board steamers for France and Belgium, but the terminus of the Lymington branch is right by the waves – just a few paces from the end of the platform to the Wightlink ferry for Yarmouth on the Isle of Wight. No Orient Express-style journey to a far-off destination here. But even so, in a hurried modern world this is an adventure in itself – to step off a train almost directly onto a boat, especially the hop across the Solent with magnificent chalky views to the Needles all the way. By pure chance there exists another pier railway just across the water at Ryde, where seventy-year-old Tube trains trundle up to meet the Portsmouth ferry at Pierhead station. As I prepare to board *Farringford* I wonder whether there can be anywhere more evocative of the slower and more genteel days of the railway than this obscure corner of south-west Hampshire. The old British Railways heritage-green livery on *Farringford*'s carriages is gently flaking and turning to rust in the salty seaside air, and soon she, like almost all her sisters, is to be retired from service.

But before setting off there's just time to have a peek around Brockenhurst, capital of the New Forest – thankfully, unlike many other country junctions, the station is not too far from the village centre. There can be few places in England where the ancient landscape has remained so unchanged. In 1079, when William the Conqueror renamed the area his New Hunting Forest, he could never have imagined that a millennium later the area would retain its timeless seclusion. The ancient system established by the Norman king to manage the woodlands and the wilderness heaths still operates today through the efforts of verderers, agisters and commoners – the judges, stockmen and land users of the forest. To this, in the present day, must be added another tribe, commuters, since fast and frequent trains up to London have turned Brockenhurst into something of a dormitory town. Although the Conqueror might feel at home among the European students, who also commute from here but to study in the many language schools of nearby Bournemouth, and who flirt multilingually in Brockenhurst's Forester's Arms, the pub over the road from the station.

As *Farringford* starts up with that reassuring *gudder-gudder-gudder* sound of old electric trains (modern ones emit a much less attractive *whee-whee-whee*) I walk through the three coaches to find they are almost entirely empty, a far cry from the very first train on the line when it opened on 8 May 1858. Decorated with laurel leaves, it was so popular that local people evicted the railway directors and bigwigs from their special carriage so that more could clamber aboard – even the footplate of the engine was packed. And no wonder everyone was so delighted. From medieval times Lymington had been a great shipbuilding centre using timber from the forest to supply the finest fighting ships to the Royal Navy. Traders landed exotic wares from all over the world on its quays, and in turn Lymington merchants exported their products, especially from the extensive saltings on the Lymington River. But by the nineteenth century trade had drifted away to Southampton as the mouth to the river silted up. The coming of the railway saved the day. No Mrs Gaskell melodrama starring Judi Dench or Jonathan Pryce here. Not a hint of a *Cranford*-style revolt against the arrival of trains in the countryside. The Lymington Brass Band played, local church bells pealed out all day long, the hundred navvies who had built the line were plied with as much ale as they could drink, and the nag that hauled the local horse bus was put out to grass for good.

One of the charms of empty trains on slow lines until quite recently was that you could do just as you fancied, unimpeded by surveillance equipment and the 'Smile, you are on camera' notices to be found in modern carriages. The old-tech forty-seven-year-old *Farringford* has an extra delight – old-fashioned first-class compartments with sliding doors and antimacassars on the seatbacks. I resist the temptation to purloin one of the kitsch 1960s smoked-glass reading lights, which could probably be hawked for a tidy sum in a Camden Town flea market, but I do sprawl back on the cushions and plonk my feet down on the seat opposite amid clouds of dust to savour the views (and yes, dear reader, I did remove my shoes).

The train leaves Platform 4 at Brockenhurst station bang on time and runs parallel with the main line for about a mile before swinging off to the south-east. We seem to go at a steady 40 mph, then slow as we climb an embankment, although we don't have to worry about signals, since the railway is operated on what is still quaintly called in train parlance a 'one engine in steam' basis – effectively as a long siding. Just one train on the track at any given time means there is no chance of bumping into anything else. There are plenty of trees on either side of the line, but once we leave the main line they disappear and suddenly we are in a barren landscape of scrubland. Seems slightly at odds with the idea of being in the heart of one of Britain's oldest forests, but the clearings are where trees have been cut down over the centuries and at least offer a chance to spot some of the famous New Forest ponies. Contrary to popular belief, the ponies are not actually wild, but owned by local people and allowed to roam freely in the forest. As we go by, a group of mares with their young, alarmed by the rattle of the train, skitter back into the cover of the forest.

The land becomes hillier and trees start to reappear on both sides of the track. We move through a succession of small cuttings as the train maintains a steady speed of around 50 mph. Not surprising then that the railway, even a century ago, was able easily to see off a rival steam-operated bus service, which appeared, in the spirit of Edwardian enterprise, in 1905. Like the races between Thomas and Bertie the Bus in *The Adventures of Thomas the Tank Engine*, the train always won because the cumbersome iron-built road vehicle frequently sank up to its axles in mud on the local rutted highways. Another rival scheme that foundered – this time for lack of money – was a plan by the flamboyant Victorian furniture entrepreneur Sir Blundell Maple to build a two-and-a-half-mile tunnel under the Solent to Freshwater on the Isle of Wight. What a disaster for the island this might have been, since one of the biggest current complaints of islanders is that their leafy lanes are being ruined by cars.

But there's a sudden interruption to my reverie. The compartment door slides open and I have a companion. This turns out to be a railwayman called Steve Upton, who tells me he has been up and down the line once already this morning. Not in his normal role as a driver of commuter trains into Waterloo, but taking a sentimental journey back in time. 'Not a busman's holiday; you could call it a train driver's holiday,' jokes Steve, jolly, bearded and in his early thirties. 'Actually, it's my day off but I wanted to come and say cheerio to these old trains that were so much part of my life. I was the first man to drive this one after it had its final overhaul at Wimbledon Depot. And where better to come on your day off for a couple of pints and a bit of sea breeze than the Lymington line?'

There's no stopping Steve. 'Marvellous what rose-tinted glasses can do,' he goes on, and I start to believe him as the *clickety-clack* of the rails and the sunny prospect through the (albeit smeary) windows summon up a hypnotic kind of nostalgia, although many former commuters imprisoned in the daily grind on these ancient and rather charmless trains would have happily have given a day's wages to consign them to the scrapyard. Most would share the view of Roger Lloyd in his essay 'The Railway Engine' that 'an electric train is fundamentally shapeless and unspectacular because its front end is in no way distinguishable from its rear end, and because of this, nobody shows the least interest when it passes'.

Steve begs to differ, telling me that when he's not driving new trains or travelling around on old ones, he runs a blog called Driver Potter which, unsurprisingly, reflects his thoughts on the railways. (It is so named because of its author's uncanny resemblance to Harry Potter.) 'This is my chance to say goodbye to a little bit of my past. Am I the only one who finds myself talking to the machinery I work with? Having spoken to other drivers, I suspect the answer is no. I know blokes who, when a train has unexpectedly reached a destination despite foul weather or some form of technical cock-up, have quietly said, "Well done, sweetheart", and patted an unresponsive console. So walking up to No. 1498 at Brockenhurst today was like meeting an old friend – the noises of the compressor thumping away under the floor, that drop in pitch from the motor generator sets whirring when the driver takes power, the *clunk* of doors and the double *clunk* of the guard's ready-to-start signal. Perhaps I'm strange, but saying "Hello, old girl" felt the right thing to do.'

'There can be few industries which include among their staff such a high percentage of people for whom going to work is just another opportunity to indulge in their favourite pastime and who go home after every shift secure in the knowledge that they have earned real folding money by doing what they like doing best,' wrote Brian Hollingsworth in his book *The Pleasures of Railways*, and Steve Upton is one of them.

'These days I drive modern trains, nothing terribly romantic – you know, aluminium coffins, airliners on wheels – but I suffer from nostalgia like everyone else, especially about the slammers. I'm filling up here . . .' He utters a mock sob. 'It's a terrible thing to find yourself being mugged in memory lane, and even more so when you suddenly realise that after many false starts this really is the last time you'll hear those sounds. The compressor will stay idle. The lights will be dark.' Steve's eyes fill with tears and he looks away, out of the window. 'Ridiculous, isn't it? It's a bloody machine! A machine that provokes a lot of memories, many of them rose-tinted with distance. But still just a machine.'

By now we're in the outskirts of Lymington. We pass through the old platform at Ampress Works station, slowly mouldering into the undergrowth. Although the station was never in the timetables, it served a large factory making piston rings – hardly a romantic product except for those who recall the days when the British motor industry was great and when a Wellworthy piston ring was an essential component in every quality

British car. There are some flood barriers on the left-hand side of the track, but the Lymington River is just out of sight behind the trees. On the other side are some suburban-looking houses and now the river appears on the left. We slow down for the disproportionately grand Victorian Lymington Town station, whose well-scrubbed brickwork gleams after a recent restoration by Network Rail. The first-, second- and third-class waiting rooms it once boasted have long gone, as has the wooden awning, which once enclosed the platform, protecting passengers from the chilly winds blowing in off the Solent, but at least there are some attractive newly installed Victorian-style lamps.

Under blue skies on this sunny morning Lymington is all quaintness and cobbles. It's not surprising that it was recently named in a Channel 5 programme 'best coastal town in the UK', winning because of its beautiful scenery, strong transport links and low crime levels. Half-close your eyes and you can summon up the seventeenth-century world of Captain Marryat's *Children of the New Forest,* which was partly set here, or the Victorian era, when Edward Gibbon, author of *The History of Decline and Fall of the Roman Empire*, was the town's MP. Lymington's High Street is a paradise for anyone seeking yachtie retail therapy with shops bearing nautical names such as Crew Clothing or the Chandlery – not surprising, since this is the home of some of the world's most famous regattas, including the Royal Lymington Cup – but what is the West Cornwall Pasty Company doing here?

For more than a century it was the railway that created the town's prosperity, but no longer. Around the station there is no sign of the busy sidings that until the 1960s accommodated the daily five-coach school train complete with locomotive that transported boys to Brockenhurst Grammar School, nor, any sign of the trucks and wagons that brought in coal, corn, cement and livestock as well as timber for boatbuilding – and took away the goods that landed on the quays. So what does

Lymington actually *do* now? Looking around, there seem to be rather too many coffee shops and retirement flats galore

The best place to ask seems to be the Ship Inn, which dominates the picturesque old harbour – all fake nauticalia and bleached wood. 'Well, there's the fishing,' says the man behind the bar, busy serving lunches to queues of impatient tourists. 'What fish do they catch around here?' 'A few mullet, I think. Got some nice fish and chips, if you want some.' (The uniform-sized battered chunks don't look particularly local to me.) 'Why don't you go to the wet-fish shop just up along the cobbles?' When I get there, Coral Bay Seafoods is closed, perhaps with good reason, since there's not too much coral in the estuary hereabouts. So I inquire in A. J. SEAL (BUTCHERS) next door. Mr Seal, straight out of Happy Families with a face as ruddy as the finest Dorset lamb chops on his counter, is happy to help. 'Do you know, you just missed my sister, who was in the shop a moment ago. She's married to one of the last fishermen in Lymington. Fish? Well, I can tell you about fish. All they catch here now are crabs, lobsters and oysters. And I'll tell you what. They send the baby oysters over to France to fatten them up and then they send them back again.' I suddenly notice Mr Seal's Union flag tie under his apron and think I'll avoid a discussion about Anglo-French relations. So I buy some lamb chops to take home. I haven't yet told him they were excellent. But I will one day.

You could walk in a trice from Lymington Town station to Lymington Pier, but why do so when you can cross the water by rail on the splendid sixty-four-metre iron viaduct, built across the harbour in 1884? So I take the next train, and what a view as I open the window! Here is a panorama of a dazzling silver forest of masts – hundreds of yachts making a gentle *chinkle-chankling* as they rock in the swell.

In the distance you get the first glimpse of the Isle of Wight, and then we arrive at Lymington Pier station. It's fairly new, as the original wooden buildings were demolished a few years ago, and has a single platform looking out onto the river on the right. On the left-hand side you can see the ferry terminal and a large car park. In front of us are the well-groomed lawns of the Royal Lymington Yacht Club. Its 2,600 members include two gold medal winners from the Beijing Olympics. The club motto is 'Successful on the water, friendly and welcoming onshore.' Make sure the pink gins are extra chilled if you want watch the legendary Thursday Evening Racing, when up to a hundred boats register to slug it out every week during the summer. Yachtie Britain doesn't come more exclusive than this.

But the not-so-posh and the bucket-and-spade brigade will have neither time nor money for such frivolities, striding straight ahead for the thirty-minute trip on the Yarmouth ferry, which is usually the shortest, calmest and most pleasant crossing to the island, although it can be brutal on a winter's day when gales whip across the water and the sharp currents at the mouth of the Lymington River make for churning stomachs. Sadly, the little branch line train no longer greets passengers with its Terrier engine at Yarmouth station. The closure of the line from Newport long pre-dated Beeching, going out of business in 1953. Local people claim it would have survived if it had hung on till now, and they are probably right.

Records of ferry services to the Isle of Wight go back to 1485, when fishermen would carry passengers between Ryde and Portsmouth, but the Lymington ferry didn't begin until 1841, predating the railway. At first it was operated by venerable paddle steamers, which were so crowded that the *Lymington Chronicle* reported the 'inconvenience and annoyance' caused by hundreds of sheep travelling on the decks with the passengers. Until 1938 cars were towed across the Solent on separate barges, promoted with a delightful poster from 1914 with a woodcut of an open-top Morris reversing down a ramp and a legend proclaiming, 'No motor tour through England can be considered complete which does not include a run round the Isle of Wight (sixty miles). Cars can be shipped by their own power, onto specially constructed boats thus obviating the necessity of lifting, and removing a difficulty, which has hitherto deterred many from visiting the lovely "Garden Isle".' Whether the London and South Western Railway should have been so assiduous in promoting the rival form of transport that killed off many of its branch lines is argued over to this day.

For decades the ferry boats were supplied by venerable British shipbuilding firms – a roll-call of the greats of heavy industry: Marshall Brothers of Newcastle upon Tyne, Robb Caledon of Dundee, William Denny of Dumbarton. It was Denny's who developed an ingenious form of propulsion which allowed the ships to move in any direction easily. This was a boon in the narrow confines of the Lymington River and led to the ships being nicknamed crabs. Today Lymington has brand-new ferries, not built on the Tyne or the Clyde but by a shipyard in Croatia. *Wight Light*, nuzzling into the jetty now and towering above the harbour, shares the service with her sister *Wight Sky*. Both vessels have facilities unheard of by those passengers who once had to rub shoulders with walking shoulders of mutton, but not everyone is happy, particularly local conservationists, who claim the new ships are churning up protected mudflats and salt marshes rich in marine and bird life.

As I wait for my service back to London at Brockenhurst, commuters are pouring off the trains from Waterloo, pasty-faced from a day in City offices and with no time to admire the nostalgic paraphernalia that has been accumulated to decorate the station. In the up platform waiting room there's a huge green enamel name board from the 1960s, rescued from the old signal box at Lymington Junction. And in the down platform waiting room there's a sepia picture of an old London and South Western Railway M7 tank simmering on the branch line in the age of steam, with a brass plaque to celebrate the

150th birthday of the Lymington branch in 2008. Here I run into Dean Pettit, a man with a badge which proclaims he is 'Station Manager, South West Trains, Solent Region'.

No plaid, brass buttons or peaked cap here. Dean, in pinstripe suit, crisp blue shirt and tie, is as spruce as the company he works for. South West Trains was the first rail firm to be privatised back in 1996 and has stayed in the same hands ever since, run with a steely personal touch by Perth entrepreneur Brian Souter, founder of the Stagecoach group. Souter, probably Scotland's most successful businessman, who founded what is now a billion-plus multinational company with a couple of second-hand buses, has sometimes courted controversy with his robust views on homosexuality and trade unions. But his Calvinism has played very successfully into his railway operations (he also runs the East Midlands Trains franchise to Nottingham and Sheffield): his trains are renowned for their cleanliness and his staff for being well turned out.

Like his boss, Dean is not given to sentimentality about the Lymington line or anything else. Not many misty eyes to be found among the executives of South West Trains. But he has time to talk, and invites me into what was once the porters' room for a very old-fashioned railwayman's cup of tea. They ran the 'heritage' trains here, he tells me, because they were convenient at the time. 'It wasn't clear whether the line would go on at all, whether it was sustainable or not. We had this rolling stock available and it kind of fitted in. We've now evolved and we've got more modern trains taking over now. It's very beautiful here and the old trains have helped raise our profile, which means it's now very sustainable. Long may it continue!'

He gets into his stride: 'People jump on the train for Lymington because it's a nice ten- or fifteen-minute journey, and look at the beautiful scenery! We'd love to put steam on, but it but it would be a logistical matter. You'd have to put a loco on each end because there's no longer any turntable or a way to run the engine round the train. I know because I'm a steam fan myself. We'd also have loved to keep the slammers – and I know they've brought in business – but they haven't got modern standards of toilets and so on.'

The trains taking over the services are, he tells me, more comfortable diesels. But how, I ask, can it make any kind of environmental sense to run diesel trains on an electrified line? The first electric trains ran out of Waterloo as long ago as the First World War. Surely that must be going backwards?

Dean is not to be thrown. 'Well, it doesn't just happen here,' he replies; 'it goes on everywhere on the railway. Diesel trains heading for Aberdeen out of King's Cross run for hundreds of miles under the wires.' And he has the perfect corporate answer: 'Modern diesels are green and environmentally friendly. And we shall be running electric services at weekends. We've not had people lying down on the tracks about the old trains going.' He laughs. 'People say it's a shame, though we're not planning fireworks on the last day. But look at this.' He holds up a head-board which one of his staff has made, ready for installation on the front of the very last train. 'Slamdoors say goodbye to the Lymington Flyer,' it reads.

In the event there were fireworks – as well as tears and many sad farewells as the final slammer disappeared into the night on 22 May 2010, bearing its specially made headboard – while the Lymington Town station manager, Ian Faletto, was presented with an inscribed tankard as a band played a suitable dirge.

Later in the year I returned to the line to see how much it had changed. The view across the Solent towards Yarmouth was as ravishing as ever, with the sea tinted golden from the setting sun way out as far as the Needles as I waited for an early-evening train from Lymington Pier. On the mainland the last rays were burnishing the walls of Hurst Castle, Henry VIII's fortress and Charles I's personal prison, which sits on a long sandy spit extending out to sea.

As it turned out, the demise of *Farringford* and her sister train *Freshwater* didn't quite bring to an end the era of the slammers on Network Rail lines. Sharp-eyed commuters passing through Buckinghamshire can still spot an old British Rail slam-door single-coach diesel railcar in the bay platform at Princes Risborough preparing to depart along the single-track branch to Aylesbury. The hawk-eyed might make a more exotic sighting of another similar train that plies up and down the Welsh valleys. More fantastically still, a group has got together to return the Brighton Belle, the world's most famous electric slam-door train, to main-line service, complete with grilled kippers for breakfast and cucumber sandwiches and fairy cakes for high tea in its luxurious Pullman saloons.

But let's get back to earth. Tonight's 17.23 from Lymington Pier is a modern Class 159 diesel railcar, whose automatic doors pop open with a judder beneath the sizeable cloud of diesel fumes hovering above us. After decades of clean electric operation, the station canopies at Brockenhurst are starting to get soot-stained again. The driver saunters from one end of the platform to the other to take the train back to Brockenhurst, and as he slings his bag in the cab, I ask how he feels about the end of the slammers. 'No skin off my nose,' he says. 'This will always be a lovely line, no matter what they run on it. But I can tell you something. There'll be tears too one day when it's the turn of this old girl to get melted down for saucepans.'

Majesty on the Orient Express: Class 8P Pacific Duke of Gloucester rests in London's Victoria station after hauling the Orient Express to Bristol and back on 27 October 2010. The modern Class 67 diesel was coupled behind to generate power for the Pullman carriages.

CHAPTER EIGHT

THE 08.45 TO BRISTOL – POIROT TAKES A DAY TRIP AS THE ORIENT EXPRESS GOES TO THE COUNTRY

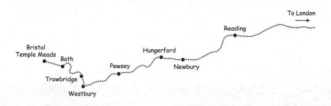

Victoria to Bath and Bristol, via Newbury, Westbury and Trowbridge

M. Hercule Poirot was a little late entering the luncheon car . . . and soon found himself in the favoured position of the table, which was served first and with the choicest morsels. The food, too, was unusually good. 'All around us are people [Poirot observed to his friend] of all classes, of all nationalities of all ages. These strangers to one another are brought together. They sleep and eat under one roof; they cannot get away from each other. At the end . . . they go their separate ways, never perhaps to see each other again.'

Thus did Agatha Christie set the scene for one of the world's most famous murder mysteries aboard the world's most celebrated train. Before the night was out one of the company had been brutally killed. Could it happen again today? With Poirot-like forensics, using my 'little grey cells', I scan my fellow passengers anticipating breakfast on the 08.45 *Orient Express* train from Victoria. No sign of anything sinister nor even a small, immaculate detective with a waxed moustache sitting in a corner. Even less a glimpse of anyone resembling David Suchet.

Perhaps this is because the *Orient Express* is taking a break from its customary itinerary delivering passengers to Folkestone for their onward journey to Paris, Venice and exotic destinations beyond. Even great trains and great detectives sometimes need a break, and today the British portion of the train is having an awayday to the country, along the old Great Western Railway main line through Berkshire, Hampshire and Wiltshire, to Bristol. But this does not mean the poshest train in the world is letting her hair down or donning some scruffy Barbour jacket. All the usual protocols are in place this morning – liveried stewards, starched tablecloths, cut-crystal glasses and silver sparkling under the Art Deco sunray lights. I am in my glad rags (or at least my best M & S suit) obeying the rules of what the *Orient Express* publicity material describes as 'The Golden Age of Travel'. 'This is one time in your life,' the official advice states, 'when you are free to look fabulous: dressing down is not our style. We suggest you wear your prettiest dress or chic suit. Leave your trainers and jeans at home as this is a day for flamboyance. For dinner, black tie is preferred.'

But it is too early in the day to contemplate such things now, as the train weaves in and out of the morning commuter services on the slow lines to the west. Bleary office-bound passengers at Clapham Junction, Wandsworth Town and Brentford, who might normally find the occasional freight train exotic, blink at this shiny apparition from the heyday of luxury travel. There's a little verse about Pullman trains by Malcolm Taylor that runs

> A Pullman breakfast
> Probably makes the most
> Perfect start to the day,
> Sliding down the west coast

On buttery kippers, tea,
Marmalade and toast

Breakfast today, on our own *Orient Express* to the West of
England, is infinitely posher: Bellinis, followed by fresh fruit
salad, scrambled eggs with chives served on a warm potato
and herb rosti, accompanied by caviar. Some commuters on
graffiti-covered platforms wave energetically even though
they may only have gulped down a hasty bowl of cornflakes
or a bacon sandwich on their way to work. 'I'm Artur,' our
steward announces in a heavy Mitteleuropa accent. 'I can get
you anything you want. I have long legs and I'm really fast.
Ladies and gentlemen, I advise you to inspect the toilets.'
Whatever can he mean? Then I remember that these old Art
Deco vehicles have magnificent terrazzo floors in the smallest
room, depicting scenes from Greek mythology.

The shiny umber and cream cars on the 08.45 (we must
not call them coaches or carriages, since their provenance is
American) are the only ones in Britain – apart from Thomas
the Tank Engine's whinging friends Annie and Clarabel – always
to have been known by names rather than numbers. I'm privileged (generally a useful word to deploy on the *Orient Express*)
to be riding in Pullman car Gwen. Even on her own, there is
enough glamour here to sum up the entire history of luxury
rail travel in the twentieth century. She started life in 1932 as
one of the original carriages on the Brighton Belle, the only
all-Pullman electric train in the world. She is packed with
sumptuous marquetry, frosted glass, sprawling armchairs – and
she boasts a working kitchen too.

You wouldn't think that all this luxury and craftsmanship was
until quite recently mouldering, rusted and waterlogged, in the
scrapyards and back gardens of Britain. Artur explains how the
Pullman cars were rescued by the American shipping magnate
James Sherwood when he formed a company to revive the old
Simplon-Orient-Express from Paris to Istanbul after the train made

its final run in normal service in 1977. Poor Gwen had suffered the ignominy of serving as the dining room of a pub in Essex.

Of the cars on the train today, only Ibis, built in 1925, ever worked on the continental service, and until Sherwood launched it in 1981 there was never a train on the British side of the Channel actually called the *Orient Express,* although British boat trains would connect with an *Orient Express* sleeping car at Calais. Nevertheless, swaying along the train through the creaking corridor connections, I pass through some of the most luxurious railway vehicles ever built in Britain – cars that transported kings, queens and heads of state – as well as rogues, spies, mistresses and the occasional murderer along the way. They served their time in a galaxy of great titled trains across Britain, all now extinct, including the Golden Arrow, the Bournemouth Belle, the Brighton Belle, the Devon Belle, the Queen of Scots, the Talisman and the Yorkshire Pullman. Cars Ione and Zena were once part of the Torbay Pullman Limited, which used to be a regular on the Great Western main line we are travelling today.

Norbert, the immaculate German train manager, shows me along the train, explaining its provenance in clipped tones, plumping the odd cushion and straightening the occasional antimacassar as we go as though it were his home – which in a sense it is, since he has been travelling with the train for a decade. He talks lovingly of the cars as though they were his maiden aunts. Ione, with her panels of burr yew and a frieze of Victorian roses, was once on the London–Edinburgh run and a favourite of royalty travelling north to their holidays at Balmoral. Lucille is distinguished by her marquetry of Grecian urns on dyed holly wood, while Minerva conveyed distinguished visitors to the Queen's coronation. Perseus formed part of Winston Churchill's funeral train, while Phoenix was a special favourite of the Queen Mother. Aboard Zena, the president of France enjoyed such a good lunch of 'Fillets of sole Zena' that he expressed his appreciation on the back of the menu card.

The steam engine on the front is a mere stripling by comparison. British Railways Standard Class 8 Pacific Duke of Gloucester was built in 1954 to the last ever design for express steam locomotives in Britain. So avant-garde was the engine that it never worked awfully well, was hated by the crews and was sent for scrap after only eight years of service. These days, like its carriages (sorry, *cars*) the Duke, as it is known, is a bit of a celebrity. Reassembled by a group of devotees out of a pile of parts from a scrapyard in South Wales, its poor-steaming problems were miraculously resolved, and today the locomotive is worth millions. But observing the Duke's lovingly polished paint, brass and copperwork this morning, I suspect its owners wouldn't swap the loco for a king's ransom.

But enough of this. You will not be surprised to learn that *Orient Express* passengers tend not to include many anoraked men clutching Ian Allan *ABC* trainspotters' guides, vacuum flasks and lapels plastered with enamel badges. Many customers don't give a hoot what is on the front of the train – in fact it is frequently hauled by a utilitarian freight diesel locomotive – and passengers may actually prefer to avoid smuts on those Valentino dresses and Paul Smith suits.

With breakfast cleared away we're already heading past Hounslow and are soon steaming into rural Berkshire. It's time to settle back in one of *Gwen*'s comfy armchairs for the views on this fine late-October day. It's been a vintage autumn, and the trees at the trackside are every shade of red, orange, russet and gold, although with a hundred tonnes of locomotive on the front we have no need to fret about leaves on the line. A word of translation here: like many trains with such a title, the *Orient Express* is something of a misnomer. The train has never run particularly fast in its lifetime, which is just as well, since the deep panoramic windows on these old carriages allow us to lap up some of the most delicious countryside in England.

We stride in stately fashion through Reading, once home to Huntley & Palmer's Bourbon Creams but now more famous for silicon chips. For several miles from here the line is kept company by two waterways, the River Kennet and the Kennet and Avon Canal. The Benedictine monastery of Douai Abbey is to the right, and to the left is a shrine of a different sort – Greenham Common, where anti-war protestors kept vigil for so long. The thirsty Duke pauses at Newbury Racecourse station to take a draught of water from a handily placed fire engine. The weed-covered platforms are quiet today, though they are normally packed on race days, when crowds throng to its popular two-mile circuit, especially for the renowned Lockinge Stakes. At Hungerford we pass over the border into Wiltshire and the rolling countryside of Marlborough Downs. To the left of the train, near Savernake, is the site of Wolf Hall, once home to Sir John Seymour, father of Jane Seymour, who became Henry VIII's third wife and mother to Edward VI. Henry apparently had many amorous adventures here. The Duke is steaming ahead in fine style now, its mournful chime whistle sending the sheep scurrying across the fields, and soon we are in the Vale of Pewsey, where it is possible to pass the time counting sheep (for there are enough of them in this rich wool country), but more fun to count the famous white horses carved on the chalk hillsides. To the left on Pewsey Hill is the White Horse of Pewsey, carved in 1785, while almost opposite is the White Horse of Milk Hill, dating from 1812. Most famous of all is the Westbury White Horse, a little further down the line. It was originally cut to celebrate one of King Alfred's victories in AD 878, and measures 166 feet from head to tail and 163 feet high. King Arthur could have set up his round table within the horse's eye, which is twenty-five feet in diameter.

But before going too far down the line, we have to report a murder. A bit late to send for Poirot, though. If it hadn't been for the assassination of Abraham Lincoln on 16 April 1845, we might not have been enjoying this the ride today. When George Mortimer Pullman, the owner of a struggling carpentry business in Chicago, read in his morning newspaper that President Lincoln was dead – shot through the brain – he spotted an opportunity. The body had to be taken from Washington to Lincoln's home in Springfield, Illinois, and George Mortimer, who had invested his last dollar in building *Pioneer,* the world's first Pullman car, at last saw a use for his creation, which had been rejected by just about every railroad in America.

Magnificent though *Pioneer* was, with inlaid walnut panels, deep-pile carpet everywhere and lavishly fitted out with brass, she was too tall, too wide and too heavy for the rails. But the enterprising Pullman went to see Lincoln's widow, put his vehicle at her disposal, and his offer was accepted with gratitude. Gangs of workmen laboured on widening tunnels, strengthening bridges and adapting depots so that *Pioneer* could travel the route. Shortly afterwards, smooth-talking as ever, Pullman persuaded Civil War victor General Ulysses S Grant to use the luxurious carriage for his triumphant journey back home to Illinois, and so one of the world's great brands was born. Although Britain's Pullman Car Company was wound up by British Rail in 1985, the name lives on, as synonymous with the sybaritic life as Hilton, Waldorf or Ritz

At Westbury we branch off northwards into the Avon valley, the river winding never far from the tracks, its banks dotted with fishermen ever hopeful of catching some plump specimen in a river which has one of the most diverse fish populations in England. Then through Trowbridge, the pretty county town of Wiltshire, birthplace of Sir Isaac Pitman, whose system of shorthand bears his name, and winding past Freshford, which played the part of Titfield in the famous Ealing comedy. Sadly the tracks of the old Bristol and North Somerset Railway, where the film was shot, are now lifted, though the capers of Stanley Holloway, John Relph and Sid James live on in the iconography of those who fought the Beeching cuts for real.

At Bathampton Junction we join Isambard Kingdom Brunel's direct main line from London into Bath. Nowhere in Britain did the builder of a railway tread so sensitively on the approaches to a city. To take his track through Georgian Bath, Brunel built a variety of bridges, tunnels and viaducts, which he designed with even greater care than usual to ensure the greatest possible degree of harmony. He had to cross the Avon twice, where it loops round the city centre, and his finely dressed masonry in Bath stone represents some of the best craftsmanship to be seen anywhere on any railway in the world. And what a magnificent vista lies before us as the line emerges from the final tunnel into Bath. Here is the city spread out in all its glory on both sides of the line, against a stage set of steep hillsides. There is even more splendour to come, as the train traverses a thirty-seven-arch viaduct before crossing St James's Bridge across the Avon on an eighty-eight-foot span, before steaming triumphantly into Bath Spa station.

It's only twenty minutes from here to Bristol, the steady beat of the *Duke*'s exhaust reverberating across the cuttings and through the tunnels. Apart from his mighty terminus at Paddington, the Grade I listed Bristol Temple Meads is Isambard Kingdom Brunel's finest masterpiece, with its castellated late-medieval-style frontage of 1840 in Bath stone, designed to harmonise with the city's historic buildings. The roof looks like the great hammer-beam structure at Westminster Hall built at the end of the fourteenth century, but typically the never-reticent Brunel had to go one better, making his own a full two feet wider. The old station shut in the 1960s and until recently housed the British Empire and Commonwealth Museum. Regrettably for Brunel fans, the shutters are now up here too, and there is only limited public access to the site, and parts of Brunel's structure serve as a car park.

Luckily, the atmospheric 'new' station, built by Sir Matthew Digby Wyatt in the French Gothic style 1865–78, has probably never been busier, bustling with roaring diesel HSTs shooting blue fumes up into the roof and suburban trains whizzing around everywhere. The station's showy tower gives even Bristol cathedral a run for its money, but more moodily ecclesiastical still is the lofty entrance hall, where it doesn't seem out of place to get down on one's knees to buy a platform ticket. No better spot to contemplate the famous joke about the link between Church and railways by the Reverend Wilbert Awdry: 'Both had their heyday in the mid-19th century; both own a great deal of Gothic-style architecture, which is expensive to maintain; both are assailed by critics and both are firmly convinced they are the best way of getting man to his destination.'

Brunel did a great service to this city, creating not only Bristol Temple Meads but the Clifton Suspension Bridge and the SS *Great Britain*, whose final resting place is a short walk away in Bristol Docks. But the man who was voted the second-greatest Briton after Winston Churchill in a BBC television survey didn't get it all right. He lost out to his old rival George Stephenson in the battle of the gauges – Brunel's 7 feet ¼ inch was wiped out by Stephenson's 4 feet 8½ inches, chosen as the rough equivalent of the width of a horse's backside in a cart. As for the world's first iron-hull propeller-driven steamer to cross the Atlantic, the old lady looks august enough, dry-docked now in the autumn afternoon sunshine. But Brunel's dream of being able to purchase a ticket at Paddington and travel all the way to New York by Great Western was doomed as the *Great Britain* was plagued by a series of jinxes. On the day of her launch in 1843, in front of Prince Albert, the champagne bottle fell short of its target and clunked into the water. Then she was trapped for a year because the dock was too narrow to extract her. Shortly after her maiden voyage, the unfortunate *Great Britain* became stranded on rocks off Ireland, only ever to make one more run across the Atlantic after her rescue.

Brunel and George Pullman, although they apparently never met, had a philosophy in common. In his epitaph for Brunel, his great friend and colleague, the Great Western's locomotive engineer Sir Daniel Gooch, remarked, 'The commercial world thought him extravagant, but although he was so, great things are not done by those who sit down and count the cost of every thought and act.' George Mortimer Pullman would surely have said hurrah to that, as it chimes so well with his famous maxim: 'Quality is remembered long after price is forgotten.'

'But isn't it all just a bit expensive?' I ask Norbert when we get back from the *Great Britain* to Temple Meads – *Orient Express* fares are four times the price of a normal ticket. 'Look around for yourself. Almost everyone on this train tonight is celebrating something – an anniversary or birthday. In an average year we get twenty marriage proposals on board. It makes people feel special.'

Meanwhile Artur and his team aboard the train are preparing for dinner on the homeward journey. Champagne corks are being drawn and a hint of roasting guinea fowl is drifting from the kitchens. Apart from the occasional burger or microwaved curry, hot food freshly cooked on conventional trains is largely a thing of the past. Almost entirely vanished now is the world described by historian Bryan Morgan in 1956: 'Diners are much-loved things, for we never outgrow our childhood amazement at refreshments on wheels. The moving sunlit countryside; the strange cries from the hell-hole of the galley; the stewards trying to steer a steady course; the times when you hit facing points too fast and everything *almost* goes for a Burton.' And whoops, it nearly happens again as the Duke pulls up sharp outside Bath and there's an almighty crash from the kitchen. Artur comes scampering down the aisle. 'Is your wine OK? Next time we 'ave funny brakes, 'old onto ze bottle.'

We're on the home stretch to Victoria now. A meal of wild mushroom soup, roast breast of guinea fowl with Savoy cabbage and caramelised onions, along with almond roulade with Bramley apple and blackberries, has been demolished. In Pullman car Gwen they're shaking the tablecloths and stacking away the silver, and in his galley perspiring head chef Jon Kahout leans against the stove, swigging strong tea from a plastic cup. 'All silver service! We keep tradition here, you know,' he says. He reckons up the tally. 'We've served 224 dinners tonight, accounting for just about every dietary fad on the way.' Further along the train his colleague Eric Salih has just washed and dried his 800th plate of the evening (no dishwashing machines in these vintage carriages). Outside, dingy inner-London stations flash by in pools of harsh sodium light. At the end of the platform at Brentford, a group of hoodies look up incredulously at this throwback to another world before staring back into their mobile phones. I recall some verses by the poet Henry Maxwell in his 'Rubaiyyat of the Railways':

> The Pullmans, with their windows wide ablaze
> And table-lamps with silken shaded sheen
> Like shop-fronts in some Eve-of-Christmas scene,
> Project a glowing beam upon the haze.

Somehow, the *Orient Express* has always been infused with an atmosphere of nostalgia for the romance of the past age of the railways. 'The great trains are going out all over Europe, one by one, but still, three days a week, the *Orient Express* thunders superbly over 1,400 miles of glittering steel track,' wrote Ian Fleming in 1956 in his James Bond adventure *From Russia with Love*. 'Under the arc lights, the locomotive panted quietly with the laboured breath of a dragon dying of asthma. Each heavy breath seemed certain to be the last. Then came another. Wisps of steam rose from the couplings between the carriages and died quickly in the warm August air . . . [the] platform throbbed with the tragic poetry of departure.'

It seems extraordinary that, more than half a century after James Bond's tussle with SMERSH, this 'great train of Europe' should still be thriving and that Gwen and Audrey and Ibis and Lucille and Zena continue to make their imperious way around the network, turning heads in the age of the Eurostar. Will they still be around in another fifty years? Don't underestimate the willpower of these plucky old girls to outlive us all.

Northern soul: Class 8F 2-8-0 No 48730 lifts a westbound
freight train across a viaduct in Burnley, Lancashire on 7 July 1968.
The Blackpool-Colne line runs through gritty Pennine scenery
along one of the historic sinews of industrial Britain. Note the
absence of motor traffic.

CHAPTER NINE

THE 08.44 FROM PLEASURE BEACH – ALIGHT FOR TRIPE, BLACK PUDDING, THE LANCASHIRE WITCHES AND THE BANDMASTER ON THE *TITANIC*

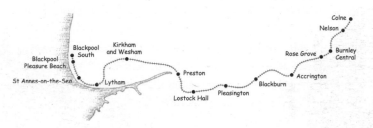

Blackpool to Colne, via Lytham, Preston, Lostock Hall, Blackburn, Accrington, Burnley and Nelson

Can there be anything jollier than arriving at a railway station called Pleasure Beach on a tram – particularly this Art Deco double-decker 'balloon car' from the 1930s? Why 'balloon'? Well, just look at her. How grand is this venerable double-deck dowager? Wouldn't you be swollen up with pride, still rumbling along the Golden Mile after all those years? You've seen off all those other icons of transport history – the Routemaster, the trolleybuses and other lesser vehicles that came and went during your lifetime. You have even outlived the steam locomotives that transformed Blackpool from a humble fishing village into one of the greatest seaside resorts there has ever been (and in its way still is). Trams have come and gone in all the great cities of the planet, but Blackpool's are destined to be here seemingly for ever.

So here we are, rumbling past the Imperial Hotel, past Harry Ramsden's chippy, past Chubbys lap-dancing club, past the little booth where Gipsy Lavinia will read your palm, past the small boarding houses with cosy names such as Jesmond Dene or Manchester House evoking working-class regions of Britain, many still advertising 'hot and cold in all rooms and spring interior mattresses' in the era of the iPad. We're cruising along, on the top deck on top of the world, aloof from everything in the modern universe, all chrome handles and green swirly-upholstered seats reeking of the 1930s – though not literally, we hope – incredibly at the beginning of the second decade of the twenty-first century. It's not a dream or some nostalgic fancy. Here is a real conductor counting out my change between taking the arms of blue-rinsed old ladies: 'Hurry along, love.' Nothing 'heritage' or retro here. It's the way folk in Blackpool have got around for as long as they can remember.

It's now more than half a century since the rest of Britain dumped its trams in favour of the 'modern' but, we have realised too late, polluting diesel bus; though many cities including London have revived them since, after recognising the error of their ways. In the meantime Blackpool can boast that its tramways never closed. Today you have to travel as far as Cairo or Hong Kong to rumble along on the top of another double-deck tram in regular passenger service.

'Nowt fancy, either,' as they say around here, about the railway journey we're about to take for fifty miles and through twenty-six stations on a slow train into the historic and spiritual heart of Lancashire, passing along the way through seemingly unremarkable towns such as Preston, Blackburn, Burnley and Nelson, and all the little places along the valleys up the branch line to Colne, coming to a premature halt in the shadow of Pendle Hill. But what riches are available on the journey, and what rewards for those who take the trouble to seek them out.

There's a famous Lancashire saying that runs, 'Beauty's only skin deep, but it's a bugger when tha' 'ast use a pick ter ger at it.' This is a railway on nobody's tourist map, yet the returns for quarrying beneath the surface are immense. It is no exaggeration to say that there are more concentrated riches mile for mile in terms of landscape and heritage than almost anywhere else in the country. But you have to 'pick ter ger at it'. It is easy to forget in the global age that it was this little bit of Lancashire that made Britain great. In these narrow upland valleys, where the soft waters ran down from the fast-flowing moorland Pennine Hills, Richard Arkwright and his steam-age contemporaries sparked a revolution that has not yet been surpassed in its impact, even by the modern potentates of the information age. The trains have long been at the heart of everything here, and continue to play their part today, where the route of the old East Lancashire Railway still holds together the thread of King Cotton, long after he has snuck away to the Third World, providing a grandstanding view – as they describe it hereabouts – of his magnificent heritage.

Our train this morning will take us past mills as mighty as palaces, though many are now converted into what hopeful local estate agents call desirable apartments for young first-time buyers – where they are not crumbling or derelict. Here too are blackened God-fearing granite churches and marble-ornamented town halls constructed to mark the power of forgotten aldermen and even more obscure civic splendours. It was one of the vergers in the blandly modern Blackburn cathedral who said to me, 'People these days are starting to forget what it all stood for. It's as though we're squatting in the remains of the Roman empire.'

Loss of empire? No single town on Britain's railway system has suffered it more tragically than Blackpool. Read and weep. Our 08.44 this morning from Blackpool South, via Blackpool Pleasure Beach, on the old Lancashire and Yorkshire main line, runs on a meagre hourly service from a single platform with a bus shelter and a buffer stop. (The timetable specifies sternly, 'No trains on winter Sundays.') Long gone are the days when the trains ran up almost to nudge the Blackpool Tower, where hordes of Wakes Week mill workers funnelled through the barriers to the smell of sea spray, chips and candyfloss. Instead, on the twenty-three-acre site where Blackpool Central station once stood, is an amusement arcade called Coral Island and a giant parking lot, one of the largest in any seaside resort in Europe. All these years later, many still shake their heads and wonder how they could have gouged the heart out of the town. Certainly when Blackpool Central shut after the Illuminations finished in 1964, an era had come to an end.

As Barry McLoughlin, historian of Blackpool's railways, put it, 'The Wakes Week holiday excursions to the coast provided a social safety valve for the toiling masses of northern mill towns. Marx and Engels could never have predicted that the enlightened self-interest of the employers would find such an ingenious way of maintaining the morale and health of their workforces.' And they all came by rail. In August holiday week 1935 more than half a million people poured through the Blackpool platform barriers. At Kirkham North Junction, where the lines divided for the three main routes into Blackpool, the signal box dealt with 600 trains in a twenty-four-hour period, an average of one every two and a half minutes. But it wasn't to last.

'On the cold damp night of 1 November 1964,' McLoughlin writes poignantly, 'the final train from Central slipped out of Platform 3 at 9.55 p.m., heading for London Euston.' Even on that last day there had been no fewer than fifty-five departures from the station. The sad spectacle was witnessed by a large crowd of enthusiasts, to the accompaniment of three detonators placed on the track as an unofficial commemoration of this historic event. More than one and a half hours later, the last train to arrive – a diesel from Manchester Victoria – approached the fog-shrouded platforms. Blackpool driver Tom Eastham sounded the hooter before being greeted with a kiss from his wife and a bottle of beer from his son. Then the station gates were locked for the final time. The following day, reported the *Evening Gazette*, the once bustling station resembled a ghost town.

What happened? For once, dark conspiracies about Dr Beeching are wrong. In his 1963 report Beeching recommended that the less conveniently situated Blackpool North station should be shut instead, and a cutting from the front page of the *West*

Lancashire Evening Gazette dated Wednesday 15 July 1964 shows there was not melancholy but rejoicing among the senior burghers of Blackpool about the closure. One 'Harry Porter, Director of Attractions and Publicity for Blackpool' was euphoric: 'It will ultimately prove to the advantage of the town,' he said in a statement. Mrs E M Hain, 'President of the Blackpool Private Hotels Association', enthused, 'I think the station's closing will prove very beneficial to Blackpool in the long run.'

Many now would argue the opposite – that the town has gone fast downhill since its direct line closed. Blowsy is one thing, folk say, but sleazy is another. Certainly, the leaders of the main political parties have thought so, since in recent times they have abandoned staging their national conferences here – not just because the Lancashire resort failed to keep up with metropolitan tastes (not too many sun-dried tomatoes and Puy lentils here) but because the facilities were so poor. But it's not all bad news. Let's hear it for Blackpool Football Club, which made its debut in the Premier League in 2010, the first time the 'Seasiders' had played at the top level for forty years. On a good day you can hear the cheers from the station here, since the Bloomfield Road ground is but a couple of penalty kicks from the station.

The rocky fortunes of Blackpool FC are perhaps symbolic of our journey today, since Lancashire's history over the past two centuries, since the first tendrils of the Industrial Revolution unfolded here, has often been a journey from triumph to disappointment and back again. Our trip today will take us through contrasting urban and rural landscapes, from bleak moorland to lush fertile meadows, from terraced towns with blue-slate roofs to postcard-pretty rural villages. We'll sweep over imposing and graceful viaducts, through dank tunnels, along lofty embankments with splendid views and through deep cuttings festooned with wild flowers amid the rusting remains of collapsed industry.

Pulling out of Pleasure Beach we soon leave the classic Blackpool whiff of chip fat and frying onions behind us. Our little two-coach Pacer diesel train is rattling along, as fast as anything built thirty years ago from old bus parts can manage. But the Pepsi Max Big One, towering above us by the shore, the second-fastest big dipper in the world, is a reminder not to get too excited about our pace. Even a century ago the trains on this line were faster, as Andrew Martin recounts in his thriller *The Blackpool Highflier*, which involves a sinister plot to derail one of the Wakes Week trains: 'Aspinall's famous Atlantic class, the Highflyers,' Martin writes,

> were 58 ¾ tons, high boiler, high wheel rims on account of 7ft driving wheels, and high everything, including speed. It was said that they'd topped a hundred many a time, though never yet on a recorded run. They were painted black like any Lanky [Lancashire and Yorkshire Railway] engine, so it was a hard job to make them shine, but you never saw one not gleaming. The Lanky cleaners got half a crown for tank engines, but it was three bob for an Atlantic.

No high flying, sing-songs or crates of Thwaites ale on board today, and certainly no record-breaking speeds either, since what was once a main line has been downgraded into what is effectively a single-track siding. But the ghosts of the good old days have not quite flown. Our first stop is Squires Gate, terminus for the tram line to Fleetwood and interchange for Blackpool International Airport (yes, really), with its flights to twenty destinations and a venerable history in the annals of aviation. As far back as 1910 pioneer aviator A V Roe, founder of Avro, transported two aircraft from Brooklands in Surrey to Blackpool by train for one of the town's early air shows. Unfortunately, as the engine struggled up an embankment near Wigan, sparks from the chimney set both machines alight.

We're now passing into posh Lancashire, stopping first at St Annes, with its genteel Victorian pier and the manicured fairways of the famous Royal Lytham and St Annes Golf Club, home to the British Open, and now Lytham itself. Even though he made his home here, comedian Les Dawson ridiculed the locals for their snobbery, claiming they 'wore sailing caps to eat their fish and chips'. The old station building is a very grand classical affair indeed, though these days open only to those seeking a meal in the restaurant into which it has been converted, rather than a third-class excursion ticket to Halifax. 'Watch out for the birds,' Andy the conductor tells me. 'And I mean the feathered kind. Not the sort we get on the hen nights round here, where the lasses drop their knickers for the price of a vodka and Coke.' He tells me that the lake just by our next stop – Ansdell & Fairhaven station, on the edge of the Ribble estuary – is home to a quarter of a million migrating and wading birds and one of the most important wildlife sites in Europe.

The Victorian junction station of Kirkham and Wesham, where the trains from Blackpool North slide in alongside us on the way to Preston, still has some of its elegant buildings and remains mired in history. Here are the traditional semaphore signals which, until the services were discontinued in the 1990s, clicked up with a clatter to give the all clear to Britain's newest and last Pullman trains, their carriages named after old-school Lancastrian gents such as Sir John Barbirolli, and Sir Stanley Matthews carrying the standard of the north-west all the way to London Euston. But no more, since the Fylde has been stripped progressively of nearly all its inter-city trains, and it is no longer possible to travel direct to London. But Kirkham remains proud home to a strand of nostalgia almost as potent as that which surrounds the railways – the British passion for biscuits. Fox's thriving factory in an old cotton mill right next to the line cannot fail to evoke thoughts of Fox's Party Rings and the comforting aura of childhood.

A broad highway of tracks appears on the left as we approach Preston station on the West Coast Main Line, with the old Tulketh Mill and its soaring brick chimney on the right of the railway a reminder of how Lancashire's county town was once the epicentre of the cotton industry. Now the University of Central Lancashire reigns supreme in the city. As well as being Britain's sixth-biggest university, it is Preston's largest employer, and you can catch a glimpse of its futuristic lime-green Media Factory on the left just before the station. Cotton factories to media factories in less than a generation. It seems hardly any time since in respectable semis up and down Britain everybody's Auntie Maude could boast that there were Horrockses finest cotton sheets from Preston crisply ironed on the bed in the spare room. In 1950s Britain Horrockses were next to godliness.

Godly, too, is the lofty church towering above the tracks, where the *parps* of the train horns and the screeches of wheels, just yards from the nave, were notorious for drowning out the Hail Marys. Sadly, there are fewer and fewer said these days in St Walburg's. Although it boasts the third-highest spire in England, at 308 feet, and the tallest of any parish church in the land, this fine Roman Catholic edifice has intermittently been threatened with closure despite its magnificent architecture and Grade I listed status. Designed by Joseph Hansom, inventor of the Hansom cab, it has a special connection with the railway. The steeple is constructed from limestone sleepers originally used on the tracks of the Preston and Longridge Railway, giving the spire an ethereal tint when reflecting the rays of the setting sun.

Also under-appreciated is Preston station, with its attractive 1880 iron roof spanning the tracks. A group of worthies commissioned by former Transport Secretary Lord Adonis recently placed it among the ten worst stations in Britain, yet others love it for its grimy, smoky and noisy atmosphere. It's a proper steam-age railway station, just as it should be, many say – not some bland appendage to a mall flogging the wares of WH Smith, Café Ritazza and Burger King. Preston – halfway between London and Glasgow – has long been famous for its refreshment rooms. From 1863 passengers were given twenty minutes to stoke up in the dining rooms, and although this is not necessary today with the sleek Scottish-bound Pendolino trains taking just over four hours from the capital, Virgin Trains still replenish their on-board catering here.

For the duration of both world wars, a free twenty-four-hour buffet service served drinks and sandwiches to anyone in uniform. Seven hundred women working twelve-hour shifts served over three million men between 1915 and 1919. Records also show that twelve million cups of tea were served between 1939 and 1945. The buffet was funded by subscription and had its own marked crockery. There is a commemorative plaque in the waiting room on Platforms 3 and 4. Today's passengers seeking refreshment at Preston might prefer to take a short walk from the station along Fishergate to find a range of Lancashire specialities in the Victorian covered market. If it is Friday, then seek out one of the delicious butter pies made from potato and onion, an old favourite in this Catholic city, where the religious could not eat meat on that day.

Don't panic, as we snake southwards over the points out of Preston, if the train appears to be heading in the wrong direction. We certainly seem to be on the wrong bridge crossing the wide waters of the Ribble as the handsome crossing of the East Lancashire Railway appears further upstream. This is because in 1968 British Railways chopped the direct line, forcing us to head west towards Liverpool before travelling east again. But Preston still boasts a quaint survivor, which can just be seen snaking up through a tunnel as we leave the station. The single-track freight-only line to Preston Docks has a fearsome 1 in 29 gradient, which in steam days would produce spectacular displays of smoke and sparks as laden locomotives struggled to get a grip on greasy tracks.

The rigid-wheelbase carriages of our Pacer protest loudly as we round the curves and cross the West Coast Main Line at Farington Curve Junction, and soon we are pulling up at Lostock Hall. Even the mention of the name of this unprepossessing former mill and mining town near the junction of the M6 and M61 sets grown men a-quiver. Do not be surprised if you see otherwise normal blokes weeping next to a weed-infested expanse of grass and concrete adjacent to the track.

For steam enthusiasts the site of the former Lostock Hall Engine Shed is the equivalent of the hallowed turf of Lords, Wembley, Anfield and Old Trafford rolled together. This was the depot that supplied the motive power for the last-ever steam trains in normal service, bringing to an end an epic era that began with James Watt, George Stephenson, Richard Trevithick and Timothy Hackworth. Even today, getting on for half a century later, many have never got over it.

A poignant notice that until recently was pinned to the wire outside the derelict site, next to a drooping cellophane-wrapped bunch of red lilies, said it all:

IN MEMORIAM. This is the site of Lostock Hall Engine Shed, built for the Lancashire and Yorkshire Railway in 1883. It was to become one of the last three sheds to service steam locomotives. On 4th August 1968, 13 locomotives left the shed to work a total of six 'End of Steam' specials, having all been cleaned and prepared the evening before by a team of dedicated volunteers. That same evening the shed was closed to steam traction after a life of 83 years. It is now more than 40 years since the men and machines of the steam era left this place. It is but a wilderness now, with nature slowly obscuring the last vestige of human industry. But our memories of the place will remain with us for the remainder of our lives. LOSTOCK HALL STEAM SHED RIP. YOU PLAYED YOUR PART RIGHT TO THE END.

'And what's more,' says Andy, as he pushes the buzzer to signal the driver to depart from an empty platform, 'the railway treated the blokes something rotten. They got a notice from the divisional manager in Preston saying their services were no longer required, without even a thank you for doing one of the dirtiest jobs in the business. Fantastic skilled men they were, but there were nowt round here or anywhere for a steam driver or a fireman, so most ended up on t' dole. Still, they've stuck together and still meet up several times a year. The lads reckon there's not a bunch of ex-employees in Britain, whether from railway, military or civvy street, who hold so many get-togethers after so long.'

All the way along the East Lancashire Railway what were once bustling goods yards, serving mills, mines and heavy industry have returned to nature. Who now remembers that the little stations along here once served some of the north's darkest and most Satanic mills? Even many of the names – Pleasington, Cherry Tree and Rose Grove – sound as though they belong to a remote little branch line deep in the heart of the countryside. But once they were euphemisms for a kind of industrial hell. The old sidings at the next station, Bamber Bridge, are submerged under a riot of July flowers. Here are the classic railway blooms of midsummer. The rosebay willowherb, with its clusters of pink spires, is a great survivor alongside the tracks. Its flowers open low on the stalk and then progressively higher and higher, so there are always blooms available for insects above the vegetation rising around. Here too is the meadowsweet, another lover of derelict railways, with its cloud-like masses of creamy flowers and sweet scent, which can just be discerned through the windows. (Give thanks for a rare train, such as this one, whose windows still open.)

Look out at Bamber Bridge for the handsome Lancashire and Yorkshire Railway signal box, dating from 1904, which controls the level crossing. Especially nice to find as most of the heritage features have been swept away from this line. Not that the Lanky was ever especially showy. 'Of all the major railway companies,' wrote John Marshall in his history of the line,

the Lancashire and Yorkshire Railway was at once the most complex and least colourful. Its plain-looking black engines, drab coaches and dingy stations hardly inspired enthusiasm and journeys on some of its former lines left an impression of short distances between dirty towns of endless industrial and residential districts. Fine country here there certainly is, but it is rare enough on the Lancashire side to arouse surprise. There was also a physical impression still remembered by those who travelled on the line as schoolboys in short trousers, caused by the indestructible horsehair upholstery which tormented their legs.

One thing the post-Beeching penny-pinchers could not remove is the magnificent engineering of this route as it sweeps across the east Lancashire valleys. We encounter the first grand structure as the train plunges down the bank to Hoghton Bottoms, at whose foot engineer Joseph Locke built the graceful three-arch Hoghton Viaduct, towering 116 feet above the River Darwen gorge. Less fortunate has been Blackburn station, the major junction on the line, where it is possible to change for slow and infrequent trains heading north to the pretty market town of Clitheroe and south into Manchester Victoria. Until not long ago there was a handsome structure here fit for the gateway to the weaving capital of the world. Even as recently as 1983, Gordon Biddle and O S Nock described it thus in their English Heritage survey of railway architectural treasures:

> Built in 1888 it has two storeys in red brick with substantial stone dressings and a central clock that sits among a variety of carved stone foliage and the letters LYR. The booking hall has been modernised without detracting from the period frontage. The main point of interest is the retention of the lofty two-bay overall roof, which covers the large one- and two-storeyed yellow brick platform buildings. Some of the windows in them still have designations such as 'First Class Ladies Room'.

But now the fine old roof has been swept away and the platforms remodelled in what you might call shopping centre, wipe-clean bland, although the listed façade and station clock survive and there is a cheery new mural by the Ormskirk artist Stephen

Charnock of eight famous Blackburn faces, including that of Mahatma Gandhi, who came here in 1931 to urge a boycott of British textiles, staying locally with a poor family of cotton workers. All highly ironic now, since three quarters of a century later Blackburn's cotton business is all but dead. A rummage through the clothing racks this morning in the old-fashioned Marks & Spencer in the centre of town reveals many a 'Made in Bangladesh' label but pitifully few things made at home. A mighty industry that began in the thirteenth century, with Flemish weavers producing their famous Blackburn check, declined from around 80,000 mills at the beginning of the twentieth century to a mere 2,000 at the end of the 1970s, fewer than John Lennon's famous '4,000 holes in Blackburn, Lancashire'.

The mill chimneys that formed a forest across the townscape like the spires of medieval churches have been felled one by one, and the confidence of Blackburn has wobbled. The heart of the town was replaced in 1979 with a giant concrete mall with ninety-one identikit shops, now looking decidedly dated. The aluminium-topped 1960s concrete lantern tower on the cathedral next to the station – looking as though it had landed on the Victorian structure from outer space – suffered from the jerry-building of the era and has had to be taken down and reassembled. Still, some things don't change. Daniel Thwaites' brewery is still there in Penny Street, two centuries after the first mashing was done, and the Thwaites shire horses can be found clopping all over Lancashire, delivering, among various brews, the highly regarded Wainwright's Fine Ale, named after the town's most famous son, the fell walker Alfred Wainwright.

Much humbled too is Accrington, once a proud junction bordered by clattering goods yards and smoking engine sheds, where services would head south to Manchester until Beeching shut them down. Still, it's hard to erase the heritage etched into every feature of this gritty landscape. Accrington's massive railway viaduct bestrides the valley, offering magnificent views of the town below. Built on a curve of forty chains radius, the twenty-one arches were originally made of brick, but it was rebuilt in stone in 1867 at a cost of £11,215. There is probably no more authentic distillation of the essence of industrial Lancashire than here, where the cast iron roof of the Victorian market hall echoes to the flat vowels and rolled 'RRRRRRs' so characteristic of this part of northern England.

At Bob's Quality Tripe and Black Pudding stall I buy my lunch – a 'Hot Black Pudding – now being served 9.30–1.30 p.m'. And where else might you be asked, 'Which would you like, love? The fatty or the lean one?' I turn down the offer of some cow heel, pig's feet, honeycomb or seam tripe but I do pick up, from the next stall, a well-thumbed copy of the Ian Allan *ABC British Railways Locomotives Combined Volume*, November 1959, its laminated corners scuffed from being stuffed into into a small boy's pockets on countless loco-spotters' outings. No doubt about the favourite locos of Peter Burton, Bridge Street, Colne, whose name is inscribed in the front cover. Here is a rich haul of motive power from the East Lancashire line, all neatly underlined – the Crabs, Austerities and 8Fs that were staples of the freight and parcels trains, leavened with some exotic express passenger engine 'cops', such as Scots and Brits.

Back at the station, one of the rare stops along the line that still has staff, a giant gleaming white Tesco supermarket has been built in the old goods yard. 'It'll do bugger all for the old market,' the booking clerk tells me, 'but at least we'll get some station toilets.' And soon we're off again through a series of former mill towns, with old embankments, sidings, the sites of brickworks, mines, power stations and coal staithes crumbling into the landscape – where they have not been built over by cheap prefabricated industrial units. Here is Huncoat, and Hapton, and now Rose Grove, with its vast empty platform, weed-grown and shorn of buildings. For most of its existence Rose Grove, the junction for the Copy Pit line, which still runs on to Leeds and York, could not have been less fragrant, with its smoking goods yards and engine sheds. But decline has brought a bonus as a luxuriant tangle of vegetation and wildflowers runs rampant.

We're now clanking over the points onto the single track of the Colne branch, mercilessly trimmed by Beeching from what was once a double-track main line through to Skipton in the Yorkshire Dales. The Victorian aldermen of Burnley would have been mortified to think that a station called Central in what was one of the grandest industrial towns of Victorian England would one day comprise a single platform on an hourly branch line service. But Burnley still has its splendid fifteen-arch stone-faced Ashfield Road viaduct, built in 1848, spanning the narrow valley of the River Calder and offering fine vistas of the town. Its future is secure since it is listed Grade II. Brierfield, the next stop, still has its Lancashire and Yorkshire Railway signal box, and the old stationmaster's house is also intact, converted into a private house and with its front gate opening onto the platform. This modest former mill town may be on nobody's map in the modern world, yet reputedly it was the inspiration for Mordor, the sinister land of J R R Tolkien's *The Lord of the Rings*. The author sometimes stayed in the neighbouring town of Fence, overlooking Brierfield, which back in the 1940s was smothered in thick layers of sulphurous smoke from the local factory chimneys, a perfect vision of an evil empire.

Squint a little and the brooding black hill shadowing us on the left of the train could just be the mountain fortress of Sauron's tower. We're not in Tolkien's Middle Earth now, but once there were evil doings in the hills round here. This is the country of the Pendle witches, a group of peasant women famously convicted at Lancaster Castle and hanged in 1612 on charges of witchcraft. Hereabouts people were said to have died in mysterious circumstances, some in great pain. Milk turned blue and cattle died without a mark on their bodies. Whether this was Jacobean hysteria, who knows, but 400 years later the witches are alive and well in the local gift shops and Hallowe'en tours. Even the bus route, the X44, is called the Witches' Way, and some of the double-decker buses are named after the unfortunate women who died at the hands of superstitious persecutors

Thankfully, the railway has remained more dignified, and now we're pulling into Nelson, with its cheery Victorian cast iron overall roof, all spick and span, gleaming glass and freshly repainted as part of a new transport interchange. We're early, and the train is nearly empty so there's a chance to chat to the driver, Angela, who tells me she is 'twenty-seven and a half' and one of only two woman drivers at Blackpool depot. Life may have moved on in the four centuries since the Pendle witches, but only relatively recently in the male bastion of train driving. 'I've been a driver for three years, but I was a conductor for five before that. I thought, if I can work at the back, then why not the front? The other drivers still look on me as a bit of a curiosity but they're quite nice, especially as I'm from London and I've learnt how to speak reet.' She laughs. 'You know – Gluss buth, not glass barth.'

Beyond Nelson the scenery becomes wilder and less industrialised, and with Pendle Hill looming mysteriously in the distance, trains cross a viaduct before entering the spartan single-platform terminus at Colne. Here, at a simple unstaffed halt, my fifty-mile mile journey from the coast comes to an end amid spectacular moorland scenery on the borders of Lancashire and Yorkshire. The town is the birthplace of Wallace Hartley, bandmaster on the *Titanic* – appropriate since it must be one of the unluckiest stations in Britain. Now a forlorn and lonely place, where busy platform, carriage sidings and engine sheds once stood, it lost its through services to Yorkshire in 1970 because of a historical quirk. The line was once a key through route between Lancashire and the West Riding, but because Colne was an end-to-end junction between two former owners – the old Lancashire and Yorkshire from Preston and the Midland Railway from Skipton – it was seen as two branch lines by the bean counters, and the Skipton services were axed in 1970.

'It's got the best case for reopening of any line in Britain,'

I'm told by Andy Shackleton, a wiry former teacher who now promotes SELRAP, the campaign group for restoring the line. a he fixes me with an evangelist's eye, and Derek, Walter and Stephen, some of the 'friends' of the line he has brought along for support, nod sagely. I meet him in the café at Boundary Mill, a vast white Xanadu-style building next to the station, which claims to be 'Britain's No. 1 factory outlet'. There's never been any love lost between Lancashire and Yorkshire folk, but the old joke that the best thing to come out of Yorkshire is the railway into Lancashire has acquired a new poignancy since there now no longer is one – at least not around here.

'Absolutely everyone backs it,' Andy enthuses. 'The case for reopening is proven beyond all doubt.' And to drive home his point he tells me about the famous 2008 Christmas Shoppers' Special from Skipton to Colne, routed via Keighley, Bingley, Shipley, Leeds, Bradford, Halifax and Hebden Bridge. By the time it wound up in Colne, this zany service had reversed three times and taken two hours and thirty-seven minutes to cover a convoluted hundred-mile route between the two towns. Which being just eleven and a half miles apart would take rail travellers a mere fifteen minutes if the line were reopened. But by now I can see a blue cloud of smoke shooting up over Colne platform, which means that Angela is firing up the engines on the Pacer, and I have to dash to be sure not to miss it. I look back, and there are Derek and Walter frantically waving goodbye. 'Look,' they shout. 'See that playing field over there? That'll be the route of the reopened line.'

Perchance to dream . . . But for now, like everyone else, I'm already heading in the opposite direction.

Holiday memories: An Ilfracombe-bound train from London's Waterloo, packed with holidaymakers, crosses the River Taw at Barnstaple behind 'West Country' class Pacific No. 34016 Bodmin in summer 1953. Now the bridge is demolished and the old line to the coast is a cycleway.

CHAPTER TEN

THE 10.20 ON THE TRACKS OF THE ATLANTIC COAST EXPRESS – IN PURSUIT OF TARKA THE OTTER

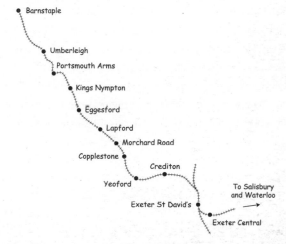

*Waterloo to Barnstaple, via Salisbury, Exeter Central,
Crediton and Umberleigh*

Can there ever have been an express train more eulogised or more mourned than the old Atlantic Coast Express? Leaving London Waterloo at 11 a.m. prompt each weekday, it was usually in the charge of one of old Southern Railway's giants of steam, a gleaming green Merchant Navy Class Pacific bearing the flag and the name of some exotic shipping line. The ACE, as it was known, was a giant in every sense of the word. The Southern's crack holiday express contained more sections than any other named train in the world, conveying its passengers to the farthest-flung coasts of north Devon and Cornwall without their ever needing to change trains.

Ranked in order along the platform to be detached in turn

down the line was a prodigious crocodile of a train: three coaches for Ilfracombe, followed by one each for Bideford and Torrington, Plymouth, Padstow and Bude, two restaurant cars and a coach for Exeter, plus vehicles for Sidmouth and Exmouth. Impressive too were the speeds. By the early 1960s the schedule for this megalith was notched up to permit mile-a-minute rates over the switchback line to Exeter, shaming the rival services from Paddington. Even as steam entered its twilight years, this was Britain's fastest ever service over a steeply graded main line, occasionally topping 100 mph.

And then the blow fell. It was announced that the last-ever ACE was to run on 5 September 1964. There was outrage in the land. The rail historian Cecil J Allen fumed, 'If ever *Ichabod* [son of Phineas in the Book of Samuel, the name meaning 'the glory has departed'] needed to be written over a once famous rail service, then this is it!' The sense of loss was infused with many different strains of nostalgia. Railway buffs mourned Britain's last-ever crack express to be regularly hauled by steam, but this was the end of another sort of era too – the British family holiday by train to the seaside, soon to be rendered almost extinct by cheap family cars and even cheaper package holidays from Luton to Lloret de Mar and Manchester to Malaga. Many on the Waterloo platform for the final service of the ACE had grown up with the famous Southern Railway poster image of a smiling little boy at the end of a railway platform, holding a suitcase and peering up at a cheery driver in his cab. The caption reads, 'I'm taking an early holiday, 'cos summer comes soonest in the South.'

Somehow that small boy was all of us, and I'm back on the Waterloo platform this bright September morning forty-six years later, trying to summon up the ACE magic. The closest we are going to get to the legendary express is today's 10.20 service to Exeter St David's. It is a nice enough train, looking splendid in the smart red, white, orange and blue livery of South West Trains, surely the most attractive uniform of the privatised rail companies. But this three-coach South Western Turbo diesel multiple unit cannot be described as grand in any sense, and looks happier among the dozens of nondescript commuter trains in the adjacent platforms rather than storming at speed along the main line.

This is actually fortunate, because the old Southern Railway route to the west is no longer a main line at all. After the knife had been put into the ACE, there followed a bloodbath of line closures on its route. Many put this down to covert Great Western Railway loyalists, lurking in the Western Region head-quarters at Paddington that controlled the line, achieving a long-held ambition to bump off their old rivals. The main line west of Salisbury was reduced to a single track and almost all the Southern Railway west of Exeter – known affectionately as the Withered Arm, because long tortuous limbs stretched into the lonely villages of north Devon and Cornwall – was chopped over the following years. Michael Flanders and Donald Swann could have worked up another couple of verses of their elegiac song 'Slow Train', with the resonant and alliterative tally of Devon and Cornwall country stations deemed to closure. Goodbye to the winding tracks to Bude and Bideford. No more would there be green carriages marked 'Waterloo' to remind Launceston and Lydford that there was a world outside. The milk churns would no longer clatter onto the platform at Halwill Junction or Holsworthy. The biggest blow came in 1970, when Ilfracombe, where just a decade earlier two loco-motives had been required to haul heavy holiday trains up the gradients outside the town, shut for ever. Here was a resort entirely created by the railway, with steep streets never designed for cars, now left marooned and trainless.

Fortunately, the loveliest line of all – from Exeter to Barn-staple – escaped the axe. True, there are no longer through carriages pulled by malachite-green West Country Class engines bearing the names of quaint villages such as Watersmeet or Westward Ho! But the ghosts of the ACE still inhabit this little railway on its thirty-nine-mile journey to the capital of north Devon. It would be cruel to call it the gnarled finger, even though that is what it now is, since here are some of the richest views from any train window in Britain as we travel along the gentle valleys of the Yeo and the Taw, through the soft rolling landscape for which Devon is famous. Let's instead call it what everybody else does – the Tarka Line, named after the epony-mous otter of Henry Williamson's famous novel, whose descen-dants still lark and dive for fish in the rivers and streams round here.

What a mercy too that the Paddington wreckers didn't manage to shut the old Southern Railway route to Exeter we're taking this morning. For the slow train traveller, the line has been transformed for the better since it escaped the axe. What was once one of the most scenic fast lines in Britain is now one of the slowest, recreating the journey as an even greater pleasure. No longer the blur of speed through the windows of express trains; now we have time to dawdle through the rolling landscapes of Hampshire, Wiltshire, Dorset, Somerset and Devon. As the essayist AP Herbert once observed, 'Slow travel by train is almost the only restful experience that is left to us'– and there are few long-distance train journeys more soothing than this.

Once past the bounds of electrified commuterland at Basingstoke, we bowl gently through Overton, Whitchurch and Andover, timeless sleepy small towns of chalky north Hampshire, with the expanse of Salisbury Plain stretching before us. Emerging from the darkness of the tunnel before entering Salisbury, there is one of the most stunning views obtainable from any train window in the land: the exquisitely beautiful fourteenth-century spire of the cathedral rising 400 feet into the sky – the highest in England, and celebrated in William Golding's famous novel *The Spire*. At the end of the platform here the thirsty locomotive at the head of the ACE would slurp from the water crane after its race down from

London, replenishing the tender before the exertions of the Devon banks ahead, which our modern Class 159 diesel train will take in its stride.

Leaving Salisbury we are into gentle meadowland alongside the River Nadder, stopping at Tisbury, where Rudyard Kipling's parents are buried, and Gillingham, not to be confused with its namesake in Kent. A prominent blue plaque on the platform states, 'On 3rd April 1856 near this spot the Hon. Miss Seymour dug the first turf for the Salisbury and Yeovil Railway, which opened on May 2nd 1859.' Miss Seymour, research shows, turns out to have been the sister of the company chairman. Could one so obscure have dreamt of such immortality? By contrast, Sir Christopher Wren, born in the village of East Knoyle to the right of the line, was destined for it.

And so we proceed via all stations, stopping at Templecombe, once the junction for the much-lamented Somerset and Dorset line, and Yeovil, famous for glove making and helicopters, where it is still possible to catch a little country train along the slow line to Dorchester and Weymouth. The ruins of Sherborne Castle, once home to Sir Walter Raleigh, can be glimpsed on a hillock by the line just before the station. What would he have made, I wonder, of the llama grazing in a field by the track? A flushed-looking man in a blazer with a severely permed and blue-rinsed wife asks me the direction of the restaurant car. I don't like to tell him that there are no longer restaurant cars as such on this or most other British trains, but I direct them to the catering trolley, and they return seemingly happy with four miniatures of Bell's whisky. After Crewkerne the train criss-crosses the River Axe at least a dozen times before pulling into Axminster, famous for its carpets as well as the little branch line that once ran to Lyme Regis, which kept the ancient London and South Western Railway Radial Tank engines in service almost to the end of steam in the 1960s, because more modern locos couldn't squeeze round the curves. The notorious 1 in 70 Honiton Bank is negotiated with ease, and soon we are sweeping past apple orchards galore, the fruit once carted by the ton to the famous Whiteways cider factory, which stood near the railway for a century until it disappeared in a corporate takeover in the 1980s.

Soon we are at Pinhoe in the Exeter suburbs, and out of loyalty to the ACE I change trains at the old Southern Railway's Exeter Central station – still there, though much humbled now. Even well into British Railways days it proudly flaunted its green signs as a reproach to the chocolate and cream of the Great Western Railway's St David's station along the line. Now towering buddleia grow between the tracks where neat flower beds once flourished, and the station carries the insignia of First Great Western, inheritors of the old GWR empire which once fought the Southern to the death on the route to the west. These days the Tarka Line service joins up with another remnant of the Withered Arm, and our two-car Pacer arrives from Exmouth, having travelled beside the beautiful Exe estuary, along the slightly obscurely named Avocet Line.

Engines whirring, we set off down the steep 1 in 37 gradient to Exeter St David's. They may hardly be exciting trains, but the Pacers, which operate nearly all the local services around here, zip up and down the bank. In steam days trains usually required a push from a 'banking engine' and quite recently a steam special stalled motionless here, holding up trains on the main line for hours. Heading north, we join the Great Western main line to London for a short while, before rattling onto the single track of the Barnstaple line at the famous Cowley Bridge Junction, with its picturesque mock-Tudor pub alongside the tracks, one of the most photographed locations on the rail network. These days it is incongruously spiced up with a prominent sign advertising Thai food.

Though all the minor stations along the way are unstaffed, and it is a long time since the last freight train ran, the Tarka Line's character is undiminished. Sandwiched between Exmoor to the north and Dartmoor to the south – with the sweet waters of the Yeo and Taw never far away – the line is famously beautiful. The unspoilt countryside, with its Devon-red soil, is enhanced by the mellow stone structures of the railway, whose platform buildings and characteristic three-arched bridges mostly survive unchanged to this day. As we head north, we may daydream and think of the line as it once was – at the heart of just about every activity in the north Devon community. As well as the through trains from Waterloo to the resorts, 'passenger trains also conveyed parcels and newspaper traffic and for some years a postal sorting office ran on the line', writes John Nicholas, the railway's historian in his book *The North Devon Line*. 'Freight traffic was heavy, with coal trains from Fremington, cattle traffic after the periodical auction markets held at almost every station, milk products from the Ambrosia factory at Lapford, timber from Chapelton and other sawmills, meat from local slaughterhouses, sweets from factories at Crediton . . . Incoming traffic included almost every necessity for local people – food, clothing, coal, animal feedstuffs, fertilisers, stone, cement, bricks and steel.'

When the trains steamed into the stations during the line's heyday, the platforms were a frenzy of activity – signalmen clanging bells and pulling levers; clerks issuing tickets, telegrams, dockets for parcels and labels for cattle and good wagons. Each station had is own permanent-way ganger and platelayers, and at night postmen from distant villages slept in bunkhouses at the stations between delivering letters to the London-bound evening mail train and collecting from the early morning down mail. Barnstaple Junction was an important railway centre employing hundreds of men, with a hundred working at the engine sheds alone.

Now the intermediate stations are mostly deserted, and Barnstaple is merely a single platform with a ticket office staffed only part of the time. We rumble through the isolated station at Newton St Cyres – no opportunity to pause at the Beer Engine pub next to the station to down a pint or two of its home-brewed Piston Bitter or Sleeper Heavy – but there's an opportunity for more genteel refreshment in the award-winning Station Tea Rooms at Crediton, the biggest town along the line, where I share a pot of tea and home-made ginger cake with Richard Burningham, formerly the stationmaster at Barnstaple, though he looks too young to have been a railway official in the days when stations were staffed. Before the train departs, there's the chance to observe one of the oldest and rarest rituals on the modern railway as drivers of passing trains exchange a token with the signalman, allowing them to proceed safely on the single track. The wood-panelled signal box built in 1875 is the last remaining on the line, and has been painted in the authentic colours of the old London and South Western Railway. 'The station was designed by no less than the Great Western's Isambard Kingdom Brunel, and once his broad-gauge tracks ran here, but it was the South Western that won the war to get the railway into north Devon,' Burningham tells me.

'I became what used to be known as chief clerk in 1985 when I was just twenty-two. I was working in the travel centre at Waterloo, and it was actually a promotion to come down here. I knew the area well because I'd come to Devon on holiday as a boy. There were many fewer trains in my time: there used to be a three-hour gap during the day. We had a bit of freight then – cement trains down from Barnstaple, for instance. But there were around 20 staff working there – even in the mid-1980s – who had moved to Barnstaple as other stations and lines shut and jobs disappeared. There was Ivor, for instance, who had spent many years as clerk at Wrafton on the Ilfracombe line. In the parcels office was George Facey, the last remaining member of staff at Ilfracombe, who was still bitter about the way the line had been run down and shut. He told how he had to turn passengers away from the through London trains in the summer because they were full.

'The line is doing a lot better now. There's an hourly service, and passenger numbers are up 11 per cent in the last year alone.' Since the end of the world of braid and peaked hats, Burningham has moved to a new base at Plymouth University, from where he oversees all the community rail lines in the south-west, and there can be no more knowlegable travelling companion as he joins me on the next train along the line to Barnstaple.

Heading north from Crediton, we slow to walking pace to negotiate the picturesquely named Salmon Pool Crossing – surely a magnet for Tarka and his family, for this is otter country, and there is no finer feast for the top predator of the river-bank than a juicy salmon or trout. 'Do you know I've never actually seen one,' Burningham admits. 'Although we have been blamed for naming the line after a leading fascist!' [Henry Williamson, author of *Tarka the Otter* was a Hitler sympathiser and a member of Oswald Mosley's British Union of Fascists, although *Tarka* has remained a much-loved classic for children to this day.] At Yeoford there are still the weed-covered remains of the busy junction where passengers once changed across the platform for Okehampton, Tavistock, Plymouth and the remote villages along the length of the Withered Arm into Cornwall. No one loved this railway more than the former poet laureate Sir John Betjeman, who wrote about its little stations in verse in his 1960 autobiography *Summoned by Bells*:

> The emptying train, wind in the ventilators,
> Puffs out of Egloskerry to Tresmeer
> Through minty meadows, under bearded trees
> And hills upon whose sides the clinging farms
> Hold Bible Christians. Can it really be
> That this same carriage came from Waterloo?

But not for much longer. After the closures at the end of the 1960s, the Withered Arm remained open only as far west as

Okehampton to serve the granite quarry at Meldon, and there is an occasional passenger train from Exeter to Okehampton on Sundays, paid for by Devon County Council. But the idea of it ever fully reopening is a pipe dream entertained by only the most daring fantasists. Meanwhile the spindly iron legs of the 120-foot-high Meldon Viaduct, which carried the line on to the far west, serve a new purpose, supporting the Granite Way cycleway and footpath that carries on to Lydford along the old rail route.

But Barnstaple beckons, and soon we are at Copplestone, where a solitary elderly lady with a shopping trolley flags down the train. At 360 feet above sea level, this is the highest point on the line and the peninsular watershed, with all the rivers to the south eventually draining into the Exe, and to the north into the Bristol Channel. Here can be seen many of the characteristic high hedgerows which flank the roads of north Devon – tall because over the centuries heavy rain has gouged out the tracks beside them. The quiet village here seems unlikely ever to have been a hotbed of militant trade unionism, but this was where Ernest Bevin, destined to become one of the legends of the Labour movement, was brought up, in a cottage called Tiddly Winks opposite the station. The boy who left school at eleven and worked for sixpence a week on a local farm eventually grew up to become a distinguished Labour foreign secretary. Curiously, the line has another connection with another giant of the Labour Party, since the son of prime minister Harold Wilson, who became a driver on South West Trains, has made a home out of the station buildings at Umberleigh along the line.

When writer Paul Theroux took the train to Barnstaple in 1983 he thought it was doomed, though 'greatly favoured by railway buffs' whose interest 'seemed to me worse than indecent and their joy riding a mild form of necrophilia'. He must have been in a bad mood, because he went on:

The landscape was motionless and silent, long low hills and withered villages – some were half dead like Copplestone, with its shut-down station and grass knee-high on the platform. This branch line was old – finished in 1854 – and it had always been useful. But it was faintly comic, as all country trains seemed as they jerked across the meadows and made the cows stare. This one was full of Bertie Wooster touches, especially in the names. It went through the Creedy Valley and on to Yeoford, Eggesford and Kings Nympton; Portsmouth Arms station was actually a public house with a funereal saloon bar and Umberleigh was probably the setting of *Jeeves Lays an Egg*.

The station names may be no less comical today, but nearly thirty years on the line's fortunes have been transformed. Our two-coach train is almost full at Morchard Road, and although there are no longer any workers arriving to pack the rice puddings at the Ambrosia factory at Lapford, there are still plenty of passengers. All trains stop at Eggesford, even though it has a population of just eighty, because this is where the north-and southbound services pass and exchange tokens for a second time. Perfect for a stroll along the platform in the sunshine while we wait for the Exeter train to arrive. All is rich and ripe and slightly over the top on this late summer's day. There's a tinge of russet about everything, and lazy wasps are lolling in the warm sun. 'From here up to Umberleigh is my favourite stretch of the line,' Burningham tells me. 'And Eggesford is the most perfect station. It was bought by the old stationmaster, and his widow still lives there. It's said the original ticket office is still untouched, just as it was when they closed it.'

We roll through the valley, past Kings Nympton and Portsmouth Arms (named after the local pub but where occasional passengers have been known to alight, thinking they are in the Hampshire naval port), past Umberleigh, with its old concrete Southern Railway sign slowly disappearing into the hedge, and tiny Chapelton, coming to rest finally at the buffers in Barnstaple after a journey time from Exeter of an hour and seven minutes. Once this was busy Barnstaple Junction, the Clapham Junction of north Devon, where local branch line trains rolled in from Torrington and Bideford, Taunton and Ilfracombe, and thronged summer Saturday trains from all over the country queued to gain access to the platforms. Now, in the words of Mac Hawkins, a photographer who travelled the old South Western system, lovingly chronicling every station then and now, Barnstaple has been 'stripped like a chicken, with only the bare bones of the carcass left'.

Still, at the end of the platform I spy a refreshment room called The Stationmaster's Café, and it is open. Can it be the same establishment that T W E Roche, the author who coined the name Withered Arm, visited after feeling hunger pangs at Barnstaple in the 1940s?

Under the single dim light, I observed a pie, the only bit of food left. The girl put it in a paper bag . . . and I took the first bite. Ugh! It would have done for a starting signal for it was bright green. But during the war you must not open carriage windows at night when the train was in motion, lest a telltale shaft of light break the blackout, so pie and I remained in uneasy company till Chapelton, when, bravely risking being mistaken for a spy hurling a hand-grenade, I flung open the door and consigned the pie to the vast hinterland beyond the platform. Like Winnie the Pooh, I began to hum a little song:

Barnstaple, Barnstaple, Barnstaple Pie
As green as grass, I wonder why
Just take a bite and you're sure to die
Barnstaple, Barnstaple, Barnstaple Pie

It cannot be the same place surely, since the plate of sausage and eggs that I order is delicious. 'Locally sourced, all of it,' proclaims the owner, an eager young man called Mike Day, who is disconcertingly similar to the TV chef Jamie Oliver. Opened in late 2008, the cafe is based in the old stationmaster's house, which had lain derelict for more than two decades, he tells me. 'It's a wonderful building. Designed by the great Sir William Tite, architect of London's Royal Exchange no less. It took me four hard years to raise the money, restore the building completely and open the cafe. We do full breakfasts – you name it – sandwiches freshly made on site, pies, pasties and sausage rolls. Did you know we've been named as one of Britain's top ten station cafes by the *Guardian*?' Just as exciting, he goes on, was when *Top Gear* presenter James May came to build a Hornby model railway track all the way from the cafe to Bideford, along the closed trackbed of the route of the ACE for his television series *Toy Stories*. 'Actually,' Day says, flashing a conspiratorial look revealing himself as a railway enthusiast, as one might do if one were a Freemason, 'the business name of my company is Atlantic Coast Express.'

Sadly, nothing bigger than a toy train will ever pass north of here again, since up ahead blocking the line is an ugly concrete structure carrying the new Barnstaple bypass. But it is still possible to puff along further – literally – to both Bideford and Barnstaple, since the trackbeds of both railways have been turned into cycle tracks known as the Tarka Trail. Hiring a bicycle in the little bike shop on the station platform, I set off in the direction of Ilfracombe, crossing the Taw by the road, since the elegant iron rail bridge was demolished in 1977, much to the chagrin of local anglers, who found it handy for catching copious quantities of bass. At low tide it is still just possible to see the stumps of the piers – a favourite perch for the cormorants, which are lined up in a row like attendants at a funeral service. As I pedal to the end of the quay a perfect little station emerges from behind some houses, track-less and frozen in time, canopies and wrought ironwork intact. This is Barnstaple Town. No mistaking it, since its old green enamel British Railways signs, complete with the characteristic 'totem' logo are still in place high up on a wall. A lady in Hunter wellingtons briskly walking a Dalmatian tells me it is now a sixth-form centre for a local school. Piles of books are stacked in the old signal box, but do the students toiling over their geography A level know that they are studying on one of the most hallowed sites in the annals of British railway history?

It was in the bay platform here that the little narrow-gauge engines of the Lynton and Barnstaple Railway began their journey, winding nineteen miles eastwards across Exmoor. There is a law of any enthusiasm, but especially of railways, that states that the more remote and inaccessible the object of fascination, the more mythical and iconic its reputation. This could not be truer of the L & B, promoted by the Victorian press baron George Newnes, publisher of *Titbits*. Built on the cheap, to a gauge of 1 foot 11½ inches, it was a lost cause from the start. The construction costs overran and it did not go near the centre of the town it served, partly, some said, from a selfish desire by Newnes to keep the railway away from his house. By the time it finally opened in 1898, it hadn't got a chance and few ever used it. The Southern Railway shut the L & B in 1935, with the closure notice sounding an oddly cheery note of relief: 'Make sure of a trip this holiday over the romantic light railway between Barnstaple and Lynton, through the beautiful scenery of the miniature Alps of North Devon . . . This line will be closed after 29 September 1935.'

The magnitude of the legend surrounding the L & B has grown in inverse proportion to the brevity of its life, and artefacts from the line today fetch fortunes at auction, while a group of diehard enthusiasts has rebuilt a section of the line near Woody Bay, inspired by their motto 'Perchance it is not dead but sleepeth.' The same sentiment can perhaps be applied to the Ilfracombe line. After Barnstaple Town the trackbed is just as it was when the rails were lifted, following a scenic route hugging the riverbank. There is even an occasional lichen-covered gradient post to remind us that trains once ran along here, and the ballast survives, still authentically soot-covered from the many thousands of steam locos that passed by in its heyday. In the almost ghostly silence of a high summer's after-noon it is possible to invoke the shades of the old Devon Belle, which once sped this way, with its fine rake of umber and cream Pullman cars and an elegant wide-windowed observa-tion coach attached to the rear. As I approach the old Braunton station I pass a man picking blackberries, whose bike panniers are chock-full of crab apples as well. 'I'm making railway jelly,' he tells me. 'Been making it for years. The best preserves always come from fruit picked on railway embankments.' I pedal on, certain in the belief that in this man's mind the railway never closed.

Past Braunton the gradients become ever more fearsome and in steam days tested the most powerful locomotives, let alone an unfit cyclist like me. On summer Saturdays the packed trains up the 1 in 37 bank at Mortehoe, just outside Ilfra-combe, required two large West Country Class Pacifics, and the sight of them storming to the summit was among the most impressive to be seen anywhere on the railways. As for me, I divert off to the coast, planning to cool off in the clear Atlantic waters at Putsborough beach. Coasting down the quiet lanes to the sea, I cross a ford and pass through the hamlet of Georgeham, where Henry Williamson spent his final days. His tiny cottage is adorned with a blue plaque. But there are no crowds of literary groupies outside the door here, since Williamson's name is still mud with the chattering classes. Nor, despite sitting in the shade by the stream for half an hour, do I spy any otters either.

Back in Barnstaple, I renew my search for the creature that everyone talks about but never seems to have seen. I buy a pint of Otter Ale in the Panniers Inn, next to the old Pannier

Market, but no one there knows anything about otters. In the Tarka Bookshop in Bear Street around the corner the assistant sells me a scuffed old copy of *Tarka the Otter* with the delicious original line illustrations by C F Tunnicliffe. 'Oh yes,' she says, 'there are otters round here all right.' 'But where can I find them?' 'Oh, I couldn't tell you that.' So I take the train up the line to Umberleigh and book in at the Rising Sun, an old fishermen's haunt just by the river, not forgetting to ask the conductor to stop the train at this request stop. (Don't worry, love,' she says. 'I won't forget you.')

'There were otters along the bank over there just last night,' David Rees, the owner's son, tells me, heaving the pub's big leather-bound fishing diary off the shelf to show me. One entry reads, 'Shared the pool with four otters last night. Wonderful experience.' Another entry reads simply, 'Bloody butchers!' Rees reckons I will be lucky to spot one, but rising before dawn next morning I creep down to the place, beneath an overhanging alder tree. The experience is almost just as Williamson described:

> Bubbles began to rise in the pool, making two chains with silver pointed links which moved steadily upstream. Twenty yards above the swirl, which lingered as the sway of constellations between black branches, a flat white head, fierce with whiskers, looked up and went under again, the top of a back following in the down-going curve so smooth that the bubbles rising after it were just rocked. Time of breathing in was less than half a second.

Tarka on the Tarka Line – who could wish for more?

On the long journey back to London later that day the setting sun in the west over my shoulder induces that delicious sense of nostalgia – happiness imbued with regret – that Atlantic Coast Express passengers must have felt returning from their Devon and Cornwall holidays. No more delicious days lingering on golden beaches for another year. Back at Waterloo, the train slips into the platform, anonymous amid the late departures to commuterland. There's no fuss and no drama. No snorting express locomotive with a grand name such as *Cunard White Star* or *Canadian Pacific* coming to rest at the buffers after its exertions. No green and silver headboard to be removed. No carriages from all over the West Country to be sorted back into the sidings. No restaurant cars to be unloaded. Our few passengers merge into the evening crowds heading for the Tube. It may not be the Atlantic Coast Express, but there is one passenger happy to have glimpsed a live otter on a still-thriving country branch line in Devon.

Branch-line beauty: Preserved British Railways 'Standard' class 2-6-0 No. 76079 crosses a bridge over the River Esk at Ruswarp, North Yorkshire, in June 2009. The 36-mile single-track line to Whitby traverses England's green and pleasant land at its most glorious.

CHAPTER ELEVEN

THE 09.36 TO DRACULALAND — A MEANDER ALONG BRITAIN'S MOST UNSPOILT BRANCH LINE

Darlington to Whitby, via Middlesbrough, Nunthorpe, Battersby, Lealholm, Glaisdale and Grosmont

There's always been a whiff of the supernatural associated with rail travel. The Edwardian tales of M R James, Britain's greatest teller of ghost stories, are full of weird goings-on involving trains. One of his most chilling stories, *A View from a Hill*, starts with an evocation of a classic journey on a slow train: 'How pleasant it can be, alone in a first class carriage, on the first day of a holiday . . . to dawdle through a bit of English country that is unfamiliar, stopping at every station. You have a map open on your knee and you pick out the villages that lie to right and left by their church towers . . .' But his fans know better than to be lulled into a sense of security; what is to follow will inevitably be the stuff of horror. In similar vein is Charles Dickens's *The Signalman*, a spine-tingling account of a spectre that haunts a railway tunnel and the ghastly consequences that ensue.

But there can be no more spooky departure in the annals of literature than that of Count Dracula from Whitby station. It was just a few yards from where I'm sitting over a coffee in the Railway Hotel near the harbour front that, according to Bram Stoker's novel *Dracula*, the world's most famous vampire left the North Yorkshire fishing port for London in one of his fifty coffins. He took the 9.30 p.m. goods train to King's Cross on the Great Northern Railway, arriving at 4.30 the following afternoon. Audaciously, he even hired the services of the national carrier Carter Paterson to make things run smoothly. Nowadays, a vast Co-op supermarket sits on the site, and I calculate that the sidings that dispatched the ghoul were somewhere near the present-day cold-meats counter. Chilling.

Stoker, an Irish-born theatre impresario, had never set foot in Transylvania, but he did stay in Whitby in 1890, where he set part of his novel. A ship runs ashore during a storm and all the crew are missing, except the captain, whose body is found lashed to the mast. A mysterious large dog jumps ashore . . . and the rest is history – or rather fantasy. But could it be that literature's most famous bloodsucker has since jinxed the railways of Whitby? Once the town benefited from four different lines: from Scarborough along the coast, from Malton on the direct route to York and London, and a twisty little track along the Esk Valley from Middlesbrough. Beeching sucked the life out of all of them, shutting the first two in 1965 and leaving the town with the least direct route and just the four daily services it has today.

As a result, Whitby must be Britain's least accessible seaside resort for rail travellers, which is why it has taken me more than five hours and two changes of train – at Darlington and Middlesbrough – to arrive here from London's King's Cross. But the compensations are rich indeed. This is a very special journey on what can be described without exaggeration as the national rail network's most unspoilt branch line. The *Sunday Times* recently described the Esk Valley line as one of the most beautiful rides in the world. 'Leaving Teesside, the train chugs out across the North Yorkshire moors, along the leafy valley through Danby, Egton and Lealholm – surely the prettiest

village in Yorkshire – to Whitby's bracing sea air, fine Geor-
giana and looming Gothic church. This is England's green
and pleasant land, writ large over 36 miles. It will make you
sigh . . .'

Sigh too over the heritage. This is a journey into the cradle
of railway history, over George Stephenson's pioneering
Stockton and Darlington Railway, where *Locomotion No. 1* helped
revolutionise the globe by hauling the first ever steam-hauled
passenger train back in 1825. Closer to Whitby, it is possible
to pass through the world's first railway tunnel, albeit on foot.
Can my modest Northern Rail Pacer service from Darlington
to Saltburn, via Middlesbrough, live up to the weight of history?
Certainly the start of the trip is grand enough. As I change off
the Edinburgh express from King's Cross, the sun is sparkling
through the glass of the magnificent semicircular roof of
Darlington Bank Top station, and the booking office clock, high
up amid the red-brick gables, signals that it is time for my
connection to depart.

Between Dinsdale and Eaglescliffe we run onto the
hallowed tracks of the first public passenger railway in the
world. But there is no bunting, no heritage park, no celebration of history, no announcement over the train's loud-
speakers that this is the gift that Britain gave to global
communications; instead there is mile after mile of the
rusting remains of the industry that once was. We rumble
past Teesside Airport station – the least used station in Britain,
where the weekly train is mostly full of gricers who like to
notch up bizarre novelties such as this. The once bustling
Thornaby marshalling yard is almost empty, with just a
couple of derelict diesel shunters and a dumped Class 56
freight locomotive with fading LOAD-HAUL insignia on the
side – sad, since most of the loads it once hauled for the
steelworks of the north-east have long ceased to be required.
At the beginning of 2010 the mothballing of the giant Corus
steelworks at Redcar ended 180 years of steel on Teesside,

although locals hope that a deal with a Thai company will get the furnaces operating at full blast once again.

But cheer up. Though most of the cranes around Middlesbrough are now lifeless, the town still has its famous Edwardian transporter bridge across the Tees, its giant stork-like legs dominating the skyline to the left of the line. The bridge's gondola suspended over the river can whizz 200 people and nine cars across the river in just ninety seconds. Hurrah too for Middlesbrough station, all high Gothic splendour with its fine nineteenth-century tiled map of the region's railways as they once were, a fitting gateway to the first town in Britain to be created entirely by the railway. 'A tribute to the greatness of Middlesbrough' was how W W Tomlinson described the station in his *History of the North Eastern Railway*.

No time to stop in admiration though, since our two-coach Class 156 Sprinter train is pulling into the platform – the Esk Valley line is fortunate in that the large numbers of schoolchildren that need the line have helped banish the ubiquitous four-wheel Pacer trains that are the staple fare on remote branches such as this. Almost nowhere else on a railway journey in Britain is the transition from gritty urban to sylvan tranquillity achieved over such a short distance and in such a short space of time. Through the window can be seen a solitary gardener grimly trying to create an allotment amid the rubble of a former dockyard, yet within minutes we shall be in a rural England mostly unchanged since Tudor times. So put the rusting remains of industrial Teesside behind you as we slip imperceptibly into the beautiful North Yorkshire Moors National Park.

Before long we are running past Gypsy Lane – not as delightful as it sounds, a rather dreary Middlesbrough suburb – and into the sleepy village of Great Ayrton. To the left, high up on Easby Moor, is the giant Captain Cook Memorial, fifty-one feet tall and twelve feet square. Cook was born in the nearby village of Marton, and the obelisk, erected by a landowner here in 1837, is inscribed:

> In memory of the celebrated circumnavigator Captain Cook, FRS, a man in nautical knowledge inferior to none, in zeal prudence and energy superior to most . . . While the art of navigation shall be cultivated among men, while the spirit of enterprise, commerce, and philanthropy, shall animate the sons of Britain, while it shall be deemed the honour of a Christian nation to spread civilization and the blessing of the Christian faith among savage tribes, so long will the name of Captain Cook stand out among the most admired and celebrated benefactors of the human race.

Phew!

Another remnant of a distant age is a huge black rocky outcrop called Roseberry Topping, which rears 1,000 feet high to the left of the railway. It is a foretaste of the difficult landscape which has allowed to line to retain its secluded charm even today. Before the railways came in the eighteenth century this part of Yorkshire was mostly wild and inhospitable – high moorland intersected by deep wooded valleys with small scattered hamlets. There was no way into Whitby except across fearsome hills. A poster for a new stagecoach service in 1794 advertises a fourteen-day journey time from Whitby to Malton, on the road to York. 'Stopping for refreshment, exercise and smoking [sic], it will run if God permits. All last wills must be made before departure.' Even today the Whitby roads are prone to winter floods and sometimes impassable.

Some passengers may well be thinking about last testaments as the train suddenly goes into reverse at the remote weed-covered platform of Battersby. But no need to fret. The direct line through here was shut in 1954 and we must perform a zigzag to head in the Whitby direction once more, passing through wild and rugged moorland, stopping at the little hamlets of Kildale and Commondale. Climbing still into Danby, the slopes here are smothered in heather, which on this early August day is turning pink and purple as far as the eye can see. This is a view once enjoyed by Katharine Parr, sixth and last wife of Henry VIII, who lived with her second husband John Latimer at nearby Danby Castle. Its remains can still be glimpsed to the right of the railway.

No one alights to enjoy the charms of the pretty village of Lealholm, but at Glaisdale there is an extended stop as the driver engages in a bizarre ritual, unlocking a grey box on the platform and extracting an ancient cast-iron key from an equally elderly cast-iron dispenser. 'Take a gander, if you like,' he tells me. 'You won't see many of these.' He explains it is a system called No Signalman Token Remote, which can only be found on a couple of other remote branch lines in mid-Wales and north Devon. Nothing digital to worry our heads about here; the system is almost as primitive as the man with the red flag who used to march in front of the early trains. Only the driver of a train in possession of the key can proceed along the line. 'But what,' I ask, 'about the trains coming in the other direction that stop at the opposite platform?' 'Oh well, the supervisor drives down once a week and swaps all the keys over.'

Between here and Whitby the track criss-crosses the Esk, sometimes hanging seemingly perilously over the water. Charles Dickens wrote, 'In my time that curious railroad by the Whitby moor was so much more curious that you were balanced against a counterweight of water and you did it like Blondin [the celebrated tightrope walker who crossed Niagara Falls].' Were this a train of the old sort with windows that open, it might be tempting to reach out and grab one of the plump trout and salmon that populate the reaches of the Esk.

Curiously there is just such a train sitting in the adjacent platform at the next station, Grosmont. Judging by the deafening hiss of steam, this is no mirage. Schools Class No. 30926 *Repton* is preparing to depart at the head of a train of Pullman coaches along the preserved North Yorkshire Moors Railway, which forms a junction here. The eighteen-mile line to Pickering – once the direct route from Whitby to York and London until Beeching cut the service in 1965 – carries around 350,000 passengers a year, figures undreamt of in British Railways days. Some reckon it to be the busiest heritage railway in the world. There are other claims to fame too: the village of Goathland, one of the line's intermediate stations, is the setting for the ITV television series *Heartbeat*, and not far from here it is possible to walk through the world's first ever railway tunnel.

'Lovely, isn't she?' says a man in an old-fashioned railway uniform festooned with brass buttons, who is lavishing a loving gaze on *Repton*. He introduces himself as Reg Blacklock, a retired history teacher from Saltburn. 'I've been a volunteer for twenty years,' he tells me. 'Beats teaching any day, this.' A neat man with a military moustache and hearing aid, he could have a walk-on part in Alan Bennett's *The History Boys*. He shows me a silver medal on his chest: 'Look, that's a North Eastern Railway Q6 Class on the enamel there. And see this whistle? A lady on a train gave me that. Look. It says LNER on the side. Must get along . . .' He departs, muttering gnomically, 'Teaching history's one thing, but not for them as don't want to learn.'

Sadly the sparse Esk Valley timetable doesn't allow me time to join *Repton* on the service to Pickering and back, so I head over the level crossing, past the little smoke-blackened stone houses of the village and along a cinder footpath to the wonderfully named Deviation Junction. At the castellated entrance to a tunnel is a notice headed: A WORLD'S FIRST. It goes on: 'You are about to walk through what is believed to be the world's earliest passenger railway tunnel. Built between 1833 and 1835 by George Stephenson as part of the Whitby to Pickering Railway, the first carriages to run through this tunnel were horse-drawn and only carried up to 10 passengers.' The 'Deviation' refers not to some unspeakable practice, but to the fact that the railway took a slightly different course through here when it became steam-operated.

This must be one of the few early railway tunnels where it is impossible to detect the ancient whiff of steam – although the tunnel is deliciously damp and cool on this muggy afternoon – but there is plenty of steam where I stumble back into the light at Grosmont Engine Sheds, home this afternoon to some giants of railway history, including the A4 express locomotive *Sir Nigel Gresley* (minus chimney) and a Somerset & Dorset Railway 2-8-0 heavy goods engine. Unlike some preserved railways, the North Yorkshire Moors has never been too bothered about trainspotter-style authenticity. Animal lovers might also enjoy the photographs of the engine shed cats Dink and Erica. Erica, fortuitously, is a tortoiseshell, which means, according to a notice, 'she is orange in line with railway regulations'. Very authentic.

Back at the Esk Valley platform, a soft rain is falling as we wait for the next departure to Whitby. Suddenly there's a moment of drama. The clerk from the North Yorkshire Moors Railway ticket office, blonde hair flying like a Valkyrie, comes rushing over to say, 'Your train's broken down at Battersby, and there won't be another along for three and half hours. But we've got a steam special running into Whitby – do you want us to give you a ride?' Whether this is brass-necked opportunism or the sort of healthy competition we all wish would happen more often on today's railways it's hard to tell. Either way, the rescue by an old steam loco of the passengers of a modern diesel is the stuff of *Thomas the Tank Engine*. Any minute now we might expect Bertie the Bus to roll down the lane. In the event, the diesel, which had been stranded by the ancient signalling system, rumbles in round the curve, and we arrive in Whitby forty-five minutes late to a round of applause from all aboard. But not before passing underneath the most impressive piece of architecture on the line, the magnificent Larpool Viaduct, which spans the valley and once carried the closed Whitby to Scarborough railway across the Esk.

The statistics are stupendous, even by Victorian standards. Built of five million bricks and costing £40,000 (a fortune in 1882), the viaduct is 915 feet long and 125 feet high, supported on thirteen arches, each with an average span of sixty feet. Even more expensive were the twisted piers, specially deflected by engineers to follow the course of the tides on the river. British Railways once put this disused marvel on the market for one pound. But it's too late for any passenger who fumbles for a coin: it now carries a cycle track, and is very popular with walkers too. More ominously the viaduct plays a part in setting the scene for evil in *Dracula*. 'This is a lovely place,' runs the opening to Chapter Six. 'The little river, the Esk, runs through a deep valley, which broadens out as it comes near the harbour. A great viaduct runs across, with high piers, through which the view seems, somehow, farther away than it really is . . .'

Who knows whether the evil vampire is responsible, but another jinx appears to be at work as I arrive in Whitby. The town is cheery and salty as usual, full of wheeling seagulls picking over the scraps from the fish market, but it is in a state of shock. The Swing Bridge, which links the east and west sides of the town across the Esk, has got stuck in the open position. Commercial life appears to have been cancelled since the town is now split in two. The broken-down bridge makes headline news for the *Whitby Gazette*, one of the classic local weekly papers that thrives against the odds, like branch lines, in regional Britain. 'It's a misery for traders,' the *Gazette* reports under the headline THE

BRIDGE OF SIGHS. 'The landlord of the Dolphin has lost £15,000 since the bridge shut.' But fishermen are doing a roaring trade ferrying people across, compensating for their morning catch, which the paper reports as 'in poor supply'.

'It's the driveshaft on the bridge that's gone,' a council worker in a yellow vest explains as he turns baffled tourists back. 'We're waiting for the parts to arrive from Italy' – a sad reflection on northern England's lost engineering heritage. What might Mr J Mitchell Moncrieff of Newcastle upon Tyne, who designed the bridge in 1908, have thought, let alone engineers Heenan and Froude of Manchester, whose other mighty achievement was the Blackpool Tower? No alternative but to seek solace in a bag of fish and chips, taking advantage of Whitby's reputation as the chip shop capital of Britain.

There's a queue of American tourists outside the Magpie Café on the riverfront, described by Rick Stein as 'Britain's best fish and chip shop'. But 'Baked cod with tapenade, wrapped in Parma ham and served in peperonata' doesn't sound quite right. Instead I cruise the back alleys in search of something more authentic. I find it in the Royal Fisheries on Baxtergate, round the back of the station, which proclaims it is run by 'The Young Fish Fryer of the Year'. I avoid the temptations of deep-fried haggis, deep-fried Mars Bars or pineapple fritters and settle for some locally caught crispy haddock. Judging by the vast quantities of mushy peas being shovelled over mountains of chips, this is clearly a backstreet favourite. These days much of Whitby's diminishing catch goes to France, where it is highly prized, and it is more than fifty years since aluminium-lined fish vans packed with ice were attached to the passenger trains at Whitby station to whizz up to London's Billingsgate market. Still, connoisseurs of vintage London and North Eastern Railway express fish wagons are able to view a preserved example at Pickering on the North Yorkshire Moors Railway.

Clutching my steaming fishy parcel, I jump aboard one of the improvised ferries and climb the 199 steps to the brooding St Mary's church, next to the ruined Whitby Abbey on the headland. It is in the graveyard here that Mina, *Dracula*'s heroine, sees the vampire attack her friend Lucy, observing 'something long and black bending over the half-reclining white figure' and catching a glimpse of his 'white face and red gleaming eyes'. One of the church vergers, sweeping up outside, spots me peering at the inscriptions on the gravestones, heavily eroded by sleety blasts from the North Sea. 'The graveyard gets ruined up here at times of the year when those goths come up here for their goth weekends. What these kids get up to on the gravestones, I couldn't begin to tell you . . .'

But I have no time to hear more, since I have a date in the Golden Lion, one of Whitby's many charismatic boozers, with Neil Buxton, who helped to rescue Whitby's sole surviving rail link by turning it into one of the first 'community rail partnerships'. Buxton, a trim bearded man in a sports jacket, is now the chief proselytiser for the branch lines of Britain in his role as general manager of the Association of Community Rail Partnerships. The 'Use it or lose it' strategy developed back in the 1990s brings together rail companies, local councils and user groups to promote the use of secondary railways. Now there are more than fifty of them around the country.

The hand of history was heavy on Buxton and the small group determined to save the line when they first met in the New Angel Inn, 200 yards from here, to plan the Esk Valley line's survival strategy, since this was the spot where in 1832, more than a century and a half earlier, George Stephenson, the father of the railways himself, had met local businessmen to organise the building of the railway. Buxton says, 'It had all been bad news for the Esk Valley even after it saw off Beeching. Up to 1965 there were forty-six staff at Whitby station, then it went down to eighteen, – and now there is not even a National Rail ticket office.' In the post-Beeching years there was much mourning as redundancy notices were delivered along the line, ending a system under which every station had a ticket office and every ticket was collected at the end of the journey and sorted back into numerical order and sent to the audit office. The arrival of a train at even the smallest station was attended by a porter, who opened and shut the doors, collected the tickets and called 'Right away' to the guard, who, after satisfying himself that all was well, showed a green flag or lamp to the driver.

This time-honoured way of life came to an end when 'pay trains' were introduced in 1969. In the 1970s most of the line was reduced to single track, and many of the signal boxes were closed. Nunthorpe, at the entrance to the line from Middles-brough, still survives. The freight services ended, and by 1988 the passenger service had been cut to seven trains a day. By 1990 this was down to four, giving Whitby its worst train service since the first steam train arrived in the town in 1847. 'In the end,' Buxton tells me, 'they rationalised it to the point where they couldn't rationalise it any further. People were deserting it in droves. There was no marketing, no sales, and it didn't deliver what people wanted.'

Since the line became a community railway, he says, passenger numbers have exploded, but there are limits to what can be achieved. For a start, there is no new rolling stock to be had for love nor money. There are fewer better demon-strations of Britain's north-south divide than the quality of the nation's trains. In the south commuters get shiny new ones, such as the Javelins which whisk London office workers to Kent at speeds of up to 140 mph. Meanwhile, all over the north of England the Northern Rail company has to beg, borrow or steal even the most ancient clapped-out carriages. 'We don't ask for much,' Buxton says.' 'The first train out of Whitby is 9 a.m. and the last one is just after seven. It would

be great if we could have an early and a late train so people
could get to work or holiday weekenders could make it here
from London.'

But things are looking up, slowly. Tonight and every other
Friday during the summer there's a very special train, laid
on by Northern Rail, that travels up to Middlesbrough and
back during the evening. Already there's a man with a
squeezebox and another with a drum kit getting on, and
crates of bottles and kegs of beer are being humped aboard
– this is the Esk Valley's legendary Music Train. Half-close
your eyes and we might have passed back into Whitby's
heyday. The old mechanical clock still bearing the legend
LNER ticks towards 7.15 p.m., and there's an unusual buzz
and bustle around the honey-coloured arches of Whitby's
handsome stone station as passengers, many with a pint or
two of Samuel Smith's or Theakston's inside them, bowl up
to take their seats. It must have been a bit like this on summer
days in the past, when jolly crowds of steel workers rolled
back to their excursion trains heading home to Sunderland
or Hartlepool.

'We time it so that people can get off at the many village
pubs along the way, take an opportunity to have a meal and get
back aboard on the way home,' says Angie Thirkell, the line's
community development officer, who has organised the train
tonight, and is busy strong-arming some bottles into the vestibule.
The list of village inns along the route where it is possible to
hop off and sup a pint or two sounds tempting. How about the
Salmon Leap at Sleights, or the Birch Hall at Beck Hole? But I
decide to stay aboard the train as we pull out past Whitby's nineteenth-century stone-built engine shed, all the infrastructure that
is left at this once-busy terminus. Not all Whitby's former industrial vigour has been spent, however. Spick and span in the shipyard on the opposite bank of the river can be seen the latest
product of the town's shipbuilding industry, a brand new trawler
called the *Virtuous*, which is to be launched tomorrow.

The evening sun burnishes the handsome stone stations on this stretch of the line, particularly Ruswarp and Sleights, built in the Tudor style by G T Andrews for the Yorkshire and North Midland Railway Company. All are in private ownership, and Sleights still retains its clock on the platform face of the building, bearing the station name and ticking away in immaculate time. Don't spend too much time watching the clock though, since there are dramatic views of the river here as it plunges through the valley. Close to the track can be spotted a small weir with a salmon stairway. For those lucky enough to catch the moment, it is a spectacular sight as the fish jump to reach their spawning grounds in the upper reaches of the river. Once there were no fish in the contaminated waters, but now the Esk is the longest river supporting the king of fish on the eastern side of the country.

By now the atmosphere is warming up, the pints are flowing and the singalongs have started under the good-humoured supervision of the conductor, John Fenwick. 'I've been doing this job for forty-seven years and I know how to keep them under control.' Suddenly there's a bang at the front and the train drifts to a halt. 'That'll be a sheep that's gone down,' says someone nonchalantly who seems used to such events. But it's a false alarm, and soon we are off again. As we get close to Middlesbrough, the light is giving out, but there is a small yellow beam to be observed inside the little wood and brick signal box at Nunthorpe which controls entry to the line. On an impulse I alight at the deserted platform and climb the stairs. The health and safety culture of the modern railway normally precludes access to signal boxes without going through a bureaucracy of permissions, but my knock on the door is answered by a tall, taciturn man, who nevertheless seems happy enough to invite me in.

He tells me his name is Mick, and he shows me around

his domain. 'There aren't many of us trained to work these old mechanical signal boxes any more,' he says, leaning against the cast iron levers, shiny with age and use. 'I'm a Grade Three, but if I were, say, at York, I'd be up there on a Grade Seven. But I like this job here fair enough. You know the best thing about it? Well, I don't have to talk to anyone. But I'm never lonely. I enjoy my own company. And keeping the railway open for the late train tonight means I'm on overtime.'

Certainly it seems comfy in Mick's little billet, with an armchair and a two-bar electric fire beneath the track diagram, where the progress of the train is tracked along the line with little magnetic stickers. There's even a magnet in the shape of Thomas the Tank Engine's Fat Controller.'I know you're thinking it's picturesque,' Mick says, 'but you should be here on a winter's day when the wind is whistling through these old wooden windows.' By now he is concentrating on the train returning from Middlesbrough, its headlights shining along the track in the dark distance. He has to set the signals and close the level crossing gates on the road outside. Apart from me, there are no passengers to join the train, although I notice there are four scarecrows attached surreally to the platform railings, one dressed as a policeman.

Back on board, the wassails are well under way. Angie Thirkell tells me, 'It's been a good one. We've got seventy tonight, so we're easily breaking even.' Thirkell, a former theatre designer, is charged with keeping up the Esk Valley passenger numbers — 'We've gone up 14 per cent in the past year' — but tonight she's also keeping an eye on Chris and Jack, the musicians, who are feverishly playing their concertina and drums, and looking after the kegs of ale in the vestibule. 'It's Wold Top, brewed in Driffield,' she tells me. 'A bright ale with a short shelf-life,' she says, mocking the seriousness of some of the real-ale buffs aboard. 'Just as well,' she giggles, 'since it's nearly all been drunk and soon we'll have to move on to the wine.'

At every little station back to Whitby the mood gets ever jollier as we pick up well-oiled folk from the village inns. Here are Rod and Eric, who've been coming on the Music Trains for seventeen years between them. They tell me they've had a 'blowout' of steak pie and mushy peas at the Eskdale Hotel in Castleton. As the musicians launch into a reprise of 'It's Now or Never', Robert and Julie are downing a bottle of Moët & Chandon with their friends to celebrate their anniversary. 'My dad was on the railway,' Julie says, misty-eyed. 'Every time we come on the train, it reminds me of him . . .' When we draw up to the buffers at Whitby at 22.11, everybody is the best of friends. People who were complete strangers at the start of the journey are shaking hands and clapping each other on the back. Chris and Jack are packing away their instruments, and Angie is crating up the empties. It's a big night for little Whitby station, able to stay up three hours later than its normal bedtime.

In the Beeching years of the 1960s bands played frequently on late trains, and there were scenes such as this all over the country, but those occasions were not celebrations; they were wakes for the very last services on branch lines shutting for ever. How thankful we must be that the beautiful Esk Valley line is still with us. Some passengers, keen to keep the festivities going, head across the road to Rosie O' Grady's, the former Station Hotel, where the magnificent North Eastern Railway mahogany clock in the bar, inscribed W Potts & Sons of Leeds, will tick away the minutes to closing time. I think of Mick, the single light shining in his solitary signal box at Nunthorpe, waiting for the train to run back up the line to the depot for the night. He'll click the ancient key token into its red cast-iron Victorian mechanism, move his little magnetic sign reading SPECIAL TRAIN along the track diagram and haul the lever until the rusty semaphore signal clatters up to give the all clear. This so easily could have been for the last time ever. We must give thanks that tomorrow morning and every other day the trains will run again on the lovely Esk Valley line, one of Britain's greatest national treasures that could so easily have been lost to us all.

All aboard the Time Train: London's Docklands Light Railway is one of the most futuristic lines in the world, yet offers a spectacular historical panorama for the window-gazer. Here one of the DLR's driverless trains pauses at City Airport station on a Bank service.

CHAPTER TWELVE

THE 09.45 BACK TO THE FUTURE – THE STRANGE CASE OF THE MISSING DRIVER ON THE DOCKLANDS LIGHT RAILWAY

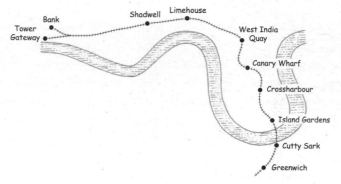

*Bank and Tower Gateway to Greenwich,
via Limehouse, West India Quay, Crossharbour,
Island Gardens and Cutty Sark*

If you mentioned the Docklands Light Railway in the same breath as the West Highland Line or the Settle and Carlisle Railway, the harassed rush-hour hordes packed on London's Bank station heading for Canary Wharf would think you had taken leave of your senses. Yet this little train ride, running along serpentine branches through east London, qualifies easily as one of the great railway journeys of the world.

No other train journey in Britain encompasses so much history and so many views for the price of a ticket costing less than a fiver, cheaper still if you buy an Oyster smartcard like a native Londoner. A trip on the DLR from Bank or Tower Gateway stations to Greenwich takes you back to the future from the Tower of London, past Dickensian riverside warehouses and the glass and concrete creations of César Pelli and Norman Foster at Canary Wharf to the elegant Greenwich of Wren, with his magnificent Royal Naval Hospital and Painted Chapel overlooking the Thames. For students of railway history there are riches to be had too. Although the DLR is London's newest rail system and one of the world's most futuristic urban transits, its lines run partly on tracks built by that great father of the railways, Robert Stephenson.

Like all the world's best rail journeys, it is the views that make the DLR so thrilling – skating over the rooftops, past the most splendid kaleidoscope of heritage to be glimpsed from any carriage window in Britain, all enriched by flashes of London's ancient river on the way. The line was built on the cheap between 1984 and 1987 to provide a quick fix for the terrible transport infrastructure through the former Port of London docks, which had moved downstream, leaving acres of dereliction behind. It started with eleven trains running eight miles to just fifteen stations. Since then, it has become one of the nation's greatest transport success stories, now carrying seventy million passengers a year to more than forty stations over twenty-five miles of network, with record levels of reliability and satisfaction. Extensions have been built to Bank, Lewisham, Beckton and Woolwich Arsenal, with yet another tentacle reaching to Stratford International for the Olympics. In the process, the DLR's ingenious engineers have burrowed three separate brand-new railway tunnels under the Thames.

But what's this? There doesn't appear to be a driver on board. Don't panic though. One of the things that makes the little red, blue and grey trains, with their tiny wheels, such fun is that they are run by computer, using one of the world's most sophisticated automated signalling systems. The trains whizz around with no human upfront, and instead of having to stop at signals are able to nuzzle up close to each other without colliding, using what is known as the moving block system. Reassuringly, there is a member of staff on board, who is usually very friendly – reflecting the high morale of everybody who works on the DLR – and willing to point out the sights. The best seats are those at the front, where in the old days a driver would sit and where you can find many a middle-aged commuter mentally pressing the start and stop buttons like a little boy.

Paradoxically, this most modern of train journeys is also a trip back in time – not just into the history of Britain but into the history of time itself, since our destination is the birth-place of chronology, the Royal Observatory at Greenwich. And where better to set off in this Tardis than at Bank station in the heart of the City of London. It was here that the very first deep-level underground railway in the world – the 'Tuppenny Tube' from Bank to Stockwell – was constructed in 1890. On the journey from Bank, deep underground for just over three miles, passengers endured trains known as 'padded cells' because of their high seatbacks and tiny windows. Why? For the sake of modernity, of course.

Perched on a ventilator outside Bank station, largely unnoticed by passers-by and sheltering a few wilted pigeons, is a statue of a fulsomely bearded man. Hat at a jaunty angle, coat casually slung over his arm, this is not a typical London statue celebrating victory and empire. 'James Henry Greathead, 1844–1896,' the inscription reads, 'Chief Engineer, City and South London Railway. Inventor of the Trav-elling Shield that made possible the cutting of the tunnels of London's deep-level Tube system.' Fast-forward the clock to the twenty-first century and I can't help feeling James Henry would have been enthralled by a journey such as mine along London's newest urban railway

Tick tock, tick tock. The passage of time in this corner of the City is present everywhere. At Nicholas Hawksmoor's grand church of St Mary Woolnoth, opposite the Greathead statue and ticking away the hours and minutes, is the clock celebrated in T S Eliot's 1922 poem *The Waste Land*, a terrifying omen of mortality for City commuters arriving at London Bridge station across the river:

> Under the brown fog of a winter dawn,
> A crowd flowed over London Bridge, so many,
> I had not thought death had undone so many.
> Sighs, short and infrequent, were exhaled.
> And each man fixed his eyes before his feet.
> Flowed up the hill and down King William Street,
> To where St Mary Woolnoth kept the hours
> With a dead stroke on the final stroke of nine.

Nowadays Eliot's clock is retired from its chiming duties and sits in the darkness at the end of the nave. The slow beat of its pendulum is a reminder to commuters who pop in for a spot of solace after hastening off the 07.23 from Orpington that it must soon be time to head on to their desks. As well as cursing the overcrowded trains that deliver them to their daily grind, the City's hard-pressed commuters might ponder the fact that it was the railway that created uniform time across the land and made us all conform to the time-driven society that regulates us today.

Until the dawn of the railway age time was calculated from the sunrise in individual towns and cities across the country, and clocks in London, Birmingham, Bristol and Manchester could differ by as much as twenty minutes. Travellers would adjust their watches as they passed from east to west, not much of a chore when a stagecoach from London to Bristol could take the best part of a whole day. Nor were people much bothered when most railways were parochial affairs. But as the network spread time began to matter, and it is not surprising that the Great Western Railway, with its main line extending east to west from Paddington to Penzance, was the first to introduce British Standard Time in November 1840.

At first railway employees would travel down the line with a portable chronometer to reset the station clocks, but soon came the invention of the electric telegraph, and an electronic impulse and a magnet were all that was needed to create the perfect timetable. Charles Dickens was one of the first to latch on, observing in 1846 in *Dombey and Son*, 'There were railway hotels, office-houses, lodging-houses, boarding-houses; railway plans, maps, views, wrappers, bottles, sandwich-boxes and timetables . . . There was even railway time observed in clocks, as if the sun had itself given in.'

Time is pressing for me too. Looking at my watch, I must make my way into the bowels of Bank station for my Docklands Light Railway train for my own rendezvous with Mean Time at Greenwich. The six-coach electric train forming the 12.45 to Lewisham looks like three trams strung together because that is how the cars were originally designed – similar vehicles run on the streets of Essen in Germany. There is no cab, and with a bit of elbowing when the doors open, I am able to nip into the front seat, ready to press that satisfying chrome lock fitting at the front that is to be my pretend driver's throttle for the journey. Eyes down, and I 'accelerate' sharply into the tunnel ahead, although curiously the train seems to manage perfectly well on its own when I take my hand off the controls. I wonder why . . .

On our way to Greenwich we follow the route of the old London and Blackwall, built by Robert Stephenson in 1840 to transport passengers to the East India Docks using an ingenious cable system with seven miles of hemp rope for each track and an ingenious winding drum at each end. There is more railway heritage nearer our destination, as we travel over the course of the little Millwall Extension Railway, opened in 1865. Who would have thought that this modest dockside track – built for horses because steam trains would have been too much of a fire risk to sailing ships – would become one of the busiest commuter lines in Britain?

The brash towers of the City are quickly left behind as we head due east, never more than a few hundred yards from the dominating presence of the Thames. Poet John Masefield described it as a 'street paved with water' and Peter Ackroyd, the great modern chronicler of London, wrote, 'It is as closely linked to the city as blood is to the body and it can be claimed with some confidence that no other capital in the world has been so dependent on its river. It was not simply its market and its port and its highway. The Thames gave London the dignity and the grandeur, the aesthetic possibilities, which it otherwise would not possess.'

Heading towards Shadwell over the old London and Blackwall viaduct, it is clear that within a few hundred yards we have passed from plutocracy to poverty, rumbling past the most deprived parts of the East End, home to one of Britain's largest Bengali communities – the latest generation of immigrants to find refuge in these parts, following the Huguenots and the Jews of eastern Europe. Colourful newly washed saris and dhotis flap over the balconies of run-down blocks of flats, while small children play cheerfully in dusty yards among stripped-down cars. To the right, on the site of the old London Docks, is Rupert Murdoch's ugly former HQ – 'Fortress Wapping' – scene of some of the most violent clashes in modern industrial history in 1986. These days News International's journalism factory, producing the *Sun*, *The Times* and the *Sunday Times*, operates from smart new offices in nearby Thomas More Square. Also at Wapping is the magnificent white shell of Hawksmoor's St George in the East church, gutted in the Blitz, though there is no longer any sign of the seedy mass of brothels, stews and gambling dens that once packed the narrow streets round here. (Samuel Johnson once urged his friend James Boswell to 'explore Wapping' so that he could better understand London life.)

But other ghosts live on. The train rides high on the arches above Cable Street, where local residents stood firm against Oswald Mosley and his blackshirts in 1936, although the old 'cockney sparrer' East End of the Krays, pearly kings and queens, 'barrer' boys and whelk stalls has almost vanished, crowded out round here by bland but pricey apartment blocks for young professionals. In Watney Street, under the railway arches at Shadwell station, that famous gor' blimey boozer, the Old House at Home, has closed, replaced by a flashy deli-catessen selling Polish groceries. Next door (but for how long?) a cockney time warp survives in Peter's Pie Shop, with its Formica tables, authentically greasy floor and large men in overalls reading the *Racing Post*. Peter's is the last of its kind in the area, and, with the trains rumbling overhead, I order that traditional East End feast of pie, mash and 'liquor' (there are no jellied eels on today) – all for £2.20. 'Yer'll have to wait for the *pay-ers*, mate, 'cos they're comin' 'ot *ay-ut* the oven,' Susan the waitress tells me in one of those old-school glottal-stopped cockney accents where vowels drop off a cliff but which, sadly, are even vanishing from *EastEnders*.

The next train east takes us deep into Limehouse, known as Chinatown in the nineteenth century, with a sinister reputation for opium dens and what were known as 'dopers' – a reputation made more lurid by the stories of Oscar Wilde and Sax Rohmer. Two Chinese restaurants linger on today, but these are respectable establishments and anyway there is a busy police station nearby. Dominating Limehouse Basin, the junction with the Thames of the Grand Union Canal and now a trendy marina, is Hawksmoor's St Anne's church, built in 1814. The clock on the tower is the tallest in London after Big Ben and was made in the same factory. Just down by the river is Narrow Street, with its attractive unspoilt eighteenth-century merchants' houses, including the Grapes pub, which Dickens wrote about in *Our Mutual Friend* and which is barely changed since he named it the Six Jolly Fellowship Porters.

As the train approaches Canary Wharf, it runs high above

the eighteenth-century warehouses of the West India Docks that are now the home of the Museum in Docklands. This is 'Blood Alley', so called because of the gashes that once scarred dockers' shoulders, rubbed raw by sacks of abrasive sugar. It's hard to imagine that here was once a vast forest of masts as far as the eye could see, in a scene evocatively described by the French novelist Louis-Ferdinand Céline as encompassing

> phantasmagoric storehouses, citadels of merchandise, mountains of tanned goatskins enough to stink all the way to Kamchatka. Forests of mahogany, tied up in thousands of piles, tied up like asparagus, in pyramids . . . rugs enough to cover the Moon, the whole world . . . Enough sponges to dry up the Thames . . . enough wool to smother Europe. Herrings to fill the seas! Himalayas of powdered sugar.

These days all that can be seen from every angle is gigantic office blocks.

But as we round the next curve, there is a truly breathtaking view. The first sight of Canary Wharf's skyscrapers from our little train is as stunning as the view of Manhattan must have appeared to generations of immigrants to America. But before we turn across the points into Canary Wharf station, with its curved overall roof looking like a miniature but modernistic St Pancras, the line rears up on a precipitous switchback. Aside from Alton Towers or Blackpool Pleasure Beach, I doubt whether there can there be such a thrilling sight to be had from the front of a railed vehicle anywhere in Britain. I lean extra hard on my imaginary driver's button to ensure we have enough acceleration to climb the gradient, and then I have to brake sharp to avoid smashing into the train stopped a few yards ahead.

Luckily, Train Captain Debbie, a neat blonde woman in a newly pressed uniform, is there to wake me from my nightmare. 'Don't worry,' she tells me. 'They rarely crash. Even when I'm driving! Though one ran through the buffers at Island Gardens once and was left dangling over the embankment. Lucky it was empty.' Debbie proceeds to explain how the trains work: 'Basically the computer keeps telling the trains to accelerate until they get to an obstacle and then they stop.' She laughs, embarrassed that it all sounds so obvious. 'I'm not very technical – I used to work in Asda.'

In a magnificent panorama through through the train window in front of us is the full megalopoloid mass of Europe's most futuristic office complex, dominated by the stainless-steel and glass of César Pelli's 1 Canada Square, for nearly two decades the tallest building in the UK until overtaken in 2010 by Renzo Piano's London Bridge Tower. Flanking it sentry-like are the smooth lines of Norman Foster's HSBC building and the equally tall Citibank headquarters, along with other corporate clones – though somehow diminished in their presence since the banking crash of 2007. In the hubristically misnamed Bank Street just by Heron Quays station is the one-time headquarters of Lehman Brothers, the biggest casualty of the 2007 banking crash, whose contents were auctioned off for souvenirs in 2010. Anyone for an entrance hall name sign at £30,000? Were the masters of the universe humbled? Not a bit of it.

There are few places in the world where it is possible to rub shoulders with so many Gordon Gekko lookalikes, since access to Canary Wharf is notoriously slow by road and no amount of money can buy a speedier journey to the City than the DLR can offer. Bankers in a hurry also throng Norman Foster's Jubilee Line station, whose entrance can be seen below the viaduct to the left. Margaret Thatcher was notoriously phobic about trains, but she personally ensured the bankrolling of the Jubilee Line extension to Canary Wharf, of which Foster's station is the greatest monument. Opened in 1999, it has been likened to a 'cathedral in concrete and glass'. At 300 metres long, it would be possible to fit another entire cathedral inside.

The grandeur swiftly peters out as the train turns south, still high on a viaduct, past the old Millwall Docks and deep into the Isle of Dogs. Technically this is a peninsula rather than an island, though the the origin of the name is unclear. Was it a place where dead dogs were washed up on the foreshore? Were the dog kennels of Edward III situated here, as some believe? In the eleventh century it was a woody marsh upon which the bishop of London kept 500 pigs. Some think it was once the Isle of Hogs, not the Isle of Dogs. What is certain is that for more than a century this was one of the most closely knit working-class communities in Britain, its population geographically cut off from the rest of London and all life focused on the river. As Peter Ackroyd writes in his book *Thames: Sacred River*, it was 'the centre of their work, most of it casual, and of their little leisure; it was their means of transport and their common sewer. It was the centre of their being, their various thoroughfares, streets and alleys leading unfailingly to the quays and stairs and other points of access to the foreshore and the dark water.' But in the 1960s and 1970s, 200 years of history passed away in a flash as containerisation took over. As Ackroyd puts it, 'The docks disappeared, vanished as if they had indeed all been a dream – the dream of toil and suffering on the banks of the river.'

Not much remains now apart from a couple of disused cranes on the dockside, frozen and immobile like dead crows. Next to Crossharbour station, beached like an old galleon among the vast new apartment blocks that provide pieds-à-terre (or sometimes love nests) for Canary Wharf bankers, is a grand old boozer, the George, still bearing advertisements for that long-extinct London favourite, Watney's ale. Outside the pub is a faded notice that reads, 'You are standing where up to 1,000 stevedores used to gather for the daily "call-on" for work in the docks. The George pub would be open from 6 a.m. to serve coffee and rum. The dock foreman appeared about 7.45 a.m. and called out the names of the men to be taken on for the next four hours. Some men only got two or three days of work a week.'

My own cockney grandfather, Tom Williams, laboured in these docks under the 'call-on' system for the whole of his life. The 'de-casualisation' of 1967 came too late for him – he died, aged sixty-four, after an accident in which a dockside load toppled on him. Would he recognise the George today? I wonder. Looking at the champagnes on the wine list and the 'Dish of the day – Chilli bake served with rocket, parmesan and garlic bread', I think not. Nor would he recognise the surroundings of the next station. Mudchute is so called because of the stinking mud dredged from the docks that was once deposited here. In time gone by the area was virtually unin-habitable; now it offers one of the most 'desirable' postcodes in east London.

But now it is time to alight from the train before it plunges into the earth towards the river and Greenwich. From the riverfront at Island Gardens station can be seen one of the finest views in the entire world. Here is Wren's creation at Greenwich in all its finery, one of the most sensational water-scapes anywhere, basking in a Canaletto-like serenity. To get across the Thames we can also plunge down into the foot tunnel, built in 1901, an eerie and chilly tube, a quarter of a mile long reached by a creaking lift. More than in any railway tunnel, there is a terrifying awareness of the dark waters rushing above your head with the potential to gush through at any moment. With a shiver, I wait for the next train.

It is a relief to resurface at Cutty Sark station. With its chippies, ice-cream emporia and souvenir shops, Greenwich is as breezy and blowsy as Brighton, and offers just as much to the curious tourist, including the Royal Observatory, the Queen's House and the National Maritime Museum. Sadly the *Cutty Sark* is out of action, hidden under a white canvas shroud following a disastrous fire in 2007. I crunch through the autumn leaves of Greenwich Park and puff up the hill on top of which the Royal Observatory is perched. Inside I climb the stairs, past the crowds of Japanese tourists snapping and posing on the Meridian Line, through the neat little quarters of John Flamsteed, Charles II's astronomer royal, up into Wren's airy astronomers' gallery, past the ingenious contraptions of John Harrison, the man who discovered how to measure latitude. And there, tucked away in a glass case, is what I am looking for – a railway guard's chronometer in a handsome brass case, marked simply 'Thwaites & Reed, London'. It was a simple device such as this – carefully borne around the network to synchronise clocks at every station, large and small – that helped bequeath time to the modern world.

No better place or moment then to end my journey and bring to a close my many thousands of pleasurable miles of travel on slow trains around Britain, undertaken for this book and its companion volume *On the Slow Train*. Fortunately there's not long to wait to get home. The hordes of tourists at Greenwich station are swept away by services that pop by every few minutes, small boys (and grown-up small boys) from all over the world marvelling that they arrive and depart without a driver, before jostling to take their own turn 'at the controls' in the front. Wherever you travel on the DLR, the trains are clean, frequent and tend to run on time. It is hardly surprising that the line has won more awards than any other railway in the land. Connoisseurs of the unusual might enjoy the fact that its operator, Serco, also administers Britain's ballistic missile early warning system as well as roadside speed cameras on behalf of the government. No wonder it runs like clockwork.

FURTHER READING

Like slow trains in the age of Beeching, Britain's small book-shops are under threat from changing lifestyles and the Internet. Enjoy them while you can. Bookshop browsing is an intense pleasure comparable to pottering along branch lines. Here is a small selection of volumes I have found useful while researching this book. Look out for them on your travels:

S K Baker, *Rail Atlas Great Britain and Ireland,* 12th edition (OPC 2010)

George Behrend, *Gone With Regret* (Lambarde Press 1964)

Alain de Botton, *The Art of Travel* (Hamish Hamilton 2002)

Gordon Biddle and O S Nock, *The Railway Heritage of Britain* (Michael Joseph 1983)

E H Cookridge, *Orient Express* (Penguin 1980)

C Hamilton Ellis, *The Trains We Loved* (George Allen & Unwin 1947)

Nicholas Faith, *The World the Railways Made* (Bodley Head 1990)

Alexander Frater, *Stopping Train Britain* (Hodder & Stoughton 1983)

David Henshaw, *The Great Railway Conspiracy* (Leading Edge 1991)

Brian Hollingsworth, *The Pleasures of Railways* (Allen Lane 1983)

Edgar Jones, *The Penguin Guide to the Railways of Britain* (Allen Lane 1981)

Alan Jowett, *Jowett's Railway Atlas of Great Britain and Ireland* (Patrick Stephens 1989)

Quentin Letts, *50 People who Buggered up Britain* (Constable 2008)

Roger Lloyd, *The Fascination of Railways* (George Allen & Unwin 1951)

Bryan Morgan (ed.), *The Railway Lover's Companion* (Eyre & Spottiswoode 1963)

Michael Pearson, *Iron Roads to the Isles; Great Scenic Railways of Devon and Cornwall; Iron Roads to the Broads and Fens* (Wayzgoose 2001, 2004, 2005)

Harold Perkin, *The Age of the Railway* (Panther 1970)

Michael Robbins, *The Railway Age* (Routledge & Kegan Paul 1962)

Wolfgang Schivelbusch, *The Railway Journey* (Berg 1964)

Jack Simmons, *The Railways of Britain* (Routledge & Kegan Paul 1961)

Gilbert Thomas and David St John Thomas, *Double Headed* (David & Charles 1963)

David St John Thomas, *The Country Railway* (David & Charles 1976)

Paul Theroux, *The Kingdom by the Sea* (Houghton Mifflin 1983)

Adrian Vaughan *Isambard Kingdom Brunel* (John Murray 1991)

Christian Wolmar, *Fire and Steam* (Atlantic Books 2007)

More publications about the railways I travelled on will be found in the lists and back catalogues of the following publishers: Ian Allan, David & Charles, the Oakwood Press and the Oxford Publishing Company. The compendious series on the branch lines and country railways of Britain published by the Middleton Press offers delightful companionship for any journey.

ACKNOWLEDGEMENTS

Special thanks to my wife Melanie, for her unflagging support and encouragement, as well as forbearance over my long absences riding the rails to the extremities of Britain. Also to my publisher Trevor Dolby for originating the idea for the book and enjoyable chats mulling over slow trains and life's other important matters. My agent Sheila Ableman has been brilliant at keeping me running to timetable. I'm indebted to Paul Bigland, Richard Burningham and Philip Haigh for reading the manuscript and for their invaluable suggestions and additions. All errors are invariably mine.

Our national passion for trains means that specialist knowledge about the railways is in plentiful supply, and I defer to those who are more expert than me. Please bear in mind that this book is not aimed at technical experts or academic historians, although I hope they might find something to enjoy in its pages and my reporter's eye has provided some fresh insights. Do get in touch with comments and corrections, which may be sent to mwmedia.uk@gmail.com. I'm grateful to Barry Atkinson, John Bearpark, John Brook, David Farrall, Alan Hakim and Clare Wilkins, who wrote suggesting amendments, which I have incorporated into this revised and updated paperback edition.

I have had generous help from people in communities all over Britain, who gave their time (and often hospitality) unstintingly in the cause of their local railway lines. A special mention for David Alder, Richard Burningham, Ian Dinmore, Brian Haworth, Gerwyn Jones, Bobby Lock, Frank and Kate Roach, Stephen Sleight, David Thomas and Angie Thirkell. I'd like to express my thanks too to the professionals of the railway industry, who helped me understand the complexities of running a railway in the modern world. Never let it be said that the current generation of railwaymen and women are any less dedicated than their forebears. Thanks to Mark Hopwood, Sue Evans and Matthew Golton of First Great Western, Steven Knight of Virgin Trains, John Gelson of East Coast Railways, Peter Meades of National Express East Anglia, Emma Knight of South West Trains, Iain Wilson and Carla Rinaldi of First ScotRail, Lindsay Marsden of Northern Rail, Anna Nash of Orient-Express, Bob Meanley of Vintage Trains and Rupert Brennan-Brown of Grand Central. I have had invaluable help from Neil Buxton and his enthusiastic staff and volunteers at the Association of Community Rail Partnerships, most notably the ever-patient Dawn Wolrich. There are others too numerous to mention, but I owe most of all to the hundreds of 'strangers on a train' I encountered mostly by chance, whose wisdom and world view helped make these journeys so enjoyable.

LIST OF ILLUSTRATIONS

Page

INDEX

(Key – NT = named train; PC = Pullman car; for all London main line stations, *see* London stations)